DO MAGIC WITH NUMBERS IN MINUTES

Numerology Magic explores the craft of divination and magic using yantra number squares. This simple yet powerful art has been practiced for over 4,000 years. Yantras are number squares as individual and meaningful as your astrological birth chart.

You can give and receive divinatory readings with yantras. Gain valuable insights into your own motivations, character, and destiny or purpose. Discover where your opportunities and passions lie, and which areas of your life may present challenges that require extra attention. Learn how to reveal compatibility between friends and lovers, and even bind lovers closer together. Create charms for all of your friends as part of the divination process.

The yantra can be used not only for divination, but worn as a talisman. The purpose of a talisman is twofold— to protect and strengthen the wearer, and to attract to the person what he or she wants. Use your yantra as a magnet to draw good things to you. Attract love, money or happiness, and greater vitality and health. Enhance your ability to make your hopes and dreams come true. More than just good luck charms, yantras are incredibly powerful energy channels for attracting your sincerest desires.

ABOUT THE AUTHOR

Richard Webster was born in New Zealand in 1946, where he still resides, though he travels widely every year lecturing and conducting workshops on psychic subjects around the world. He has written many books, mainly on psychic subjects, and also writes monthly magazine columns.

Richard is married with three children. His family is very supportive of the way Richard makes his living, but his older son, after watching his father's career, has decided to become an accountant.

TO WRITE TO THE AUTHOR

If you wish to contact the author or would like more information about this book, please write to the author in care of Llewellyn Worldwide, and we will forward your request. Both the author and publisher appreciate hearing from you and learning of your enjoyment of this book and how it has helped you. Llewellyn Worldwide cannot guarantee that every letter written to the author can be answered, but all will be forwarded. Please write to:

Richard Webster
c/o Llewellyn Worldwide
P.O. Box 64383, Dept. K813-3,
St. Paul, MN 55164-0383, U.S.A.
Please enclose a self-addressed, stamped envelope for reply,
or $1.00 to cover costs.
If outside the U.S.A., enclose international postal reply coupon.

⌗ ◇ ⌗

numerology
Magic

Use number Squares for
Love, Luck & Protection

⌗ ◇ ⌗

Richard Webster

1999
Llewellyn Publications
St. Paul, Minnesota, U.S.A. 55164-0383

SECOND EDITION
Second printing, 1999
(Previously titled *Talisman Magic*)

First edition, one printing, 1995

Cover design by Lisa Novak
Book design, layout, and editing by Susan Van Sant

Library of Congress Cataloging-in-Publication Data
Webster, Richard, 1946–
    Numerology magic : use number squares for love, luck & protection / Richard Webster. --2nd ed.
       p.   cm.
  Rev. ed. of: Talisman magic
    Includes bibliographical references (p. 161) and index.
    ISBN 1-56718-813-3 (pbk.)
    1. Magic. 2. Talismans. 3. Yantras. 4. Magic squares.
  I. Webster, Richard, 1946-   Talisman magic. II. Title.
BF1611.W43 1999
133.4'3--dc21   98-35459
                                                  CIP

Llewellyn Publications
A Division of Llewellyn Worldwide, Ltd.
P.O. 64383, St. Paul, MN 55164-0383
www.llewellyn.com

Printed in the United States of America

OTHER BOOKS BY RICHARD WEBSTER
(Published by Llewellyn Publications)

Revealing Hands: How to Read Palms

Omens, Oghams & Oracles: Divination in the Druidic Tradition

Dowsing for Beginners: The Art of Discovering Water, Treasure, Gold, Oil, Artifacts

Feng Shui for Beginners

Seven Secrets to Success: A Story of Hope

Aura Reading for Beginners

Astral Travel for Beginners

Spirit Guides & Angel Guardians

Chinese Numerology

101 Feng Shui Tips for the Home

Feng Shui for Apartment Living

Feng Shui for the Workplace

Feng Shui for Love and Romance

Feng Shui in the Garden

Feng Shui for Success and Happiness

ACKNOWLEDGMENTS

Many people, all around the world, have helped me over the years with my study of magic squares and yantras.

I'd particularly like to thank:

> Mr. S. K. Ghai, Mr. L. R. Chawdhri, and Mr. J. K. Sastri in India;

> Bob Mason, Carl Herron, Docc Hilford, David Alexander, Ron Martin, Mark Strivings, and the late Orville Meyer in the United States;

> Jon Kealoha in Hawaii;

> Craige McComb Snader in Mexico;

> T'ai Lau in Hong Kong;

> and Peter Graham, Alan Watson, and Jeff Martin in New Zealand.

This book is dedicated, with my grateful thanks, to all of the above.

TABLE OF CONTENTS

Introduction / xi

CHAPTER ONE: Yantras / 1

CHAPTER TWO: Magic Squares / 11

CHAPTER THREE: The Amazing Square of Wu / 19

CHAPTER FOUR: Your Personal Yantra / 41

CHAPTER FIVE: The Meanings of Each Box / 49

CHAPTER SIX: The Meanings of the Numbers / 53

CHAPTER SEVEN: Box "D" – The Destiny Number / 59

CHAPTER EIGHT: The Other Boxes / 65

CHAPTER NINE: Reading the Yantra / 99

CHAPTER TEN: Into the Future / 107

CHAPTER ELEVEN: Love and Compatibility / 115

CHAPTER TWELVE: Money / 131

CHAPTER THIRTEEN: Yantras in India / 137

CHAPTER FOURTEEN: Talismans / 147

CHAPTER FIFTEEN: Conclusion / 155

Endnotes / 157

Bibliography and Suggested Reading / 161

Index / 165

INTRODUCTION

It was a hot, steamy day in New Delhi. I was in a motorized rickshaw heading for Connaught Place in the middle of the city. Traffic noise and fumes engulfed me as the little rickshaw maneuvered around a large roundabout. Halfway around, an ancient truck headed straight for us and my driver had to rapidly brake and swerve to the right to avoid a collision. My driver shook his fist and yelled at the truck driver. Traffic behind us became impatient and, after transferring his shouts to the people stuck behind us, my driver started his machine again. I noticed that for the rest of the ride my driver clutched something hanging from his neck.

While paying him I asked what it was he had been holding so tightly. With an embarrassed laugh he told me it was his yantra. I was familiar with pictorial yantras and asked if I could see it. From a dirty leather pouch hung around his neck he produced a grimy piece of paper, which he unfolded and showed me. It was a magic square, not what I expected at all.

"Why do you wear it?" I asked, even though I thought I knew the answer.

"For luck," he replied. "And for protection."

"Thank you," I said. "Thank you very much."

I stood on the pavement watching him drive away and thought of all the questions I should have asked. It would have saved me a lot of time.

I was familiar with magic squares. For one year in high school I had a brilliant mathematics teacher. Mr. Temple used to entertain us on Friday afternoons with a variety of mathematical puzzles, such as proving that $1 = 2$. One Friday he constructed a magic square for us and I was so impressed that I copied it down and took it home to show to my parents. But magic squares weren't yantras! Or were they?

It took me a couple of days to find the answer. I could find nothing on yantras in the New Delhi bookstores. I asked at my hotel for the names of some numerologists. The clerk there either did not understand the question or did not know of any. Fortunately, a palmist I knew was more helpful. Not only did he have some books on yantras, but he also arranged for me to meet a Mr. Sastri who worked as a consulting numerologist.

Unfortunately, Mr. Sastri's knowledge of English was limited and it was hard to understand much of what he told me. He was delighted to talk with me and we spent several afternoons discussing the subject. The books were helpful, also, but were overly fatalistic to my mind. Gradually, over a period of time, my knowledge grew and I have been constructing and interpreting yantras for my clients for some ten years now.

A magic square consists of a series of numbers arranged in such a way that all of the rows, columns, and diagonals add up to the same number. Some magic squares add up to the same number in more than forty different ways.

Yantras are a specific type of magic square that are constructed for a specific talismanic or divinational purpose. This is how magic squares began in the first place. Originally, all magic squares were yantras. However, in the last two hundred years, mathematicians discovered that they enjoyed constructing different types of magic squares. Many of them would have no idea how they originated in the first place. A friend of mine is obsessed with constructing the largest magic square in the world. He is working on this purely for fun. The finished square will give him pleasure and satisfaction, and that is his sole interest in the subject. I have tried to talk to him about yantras, as distinct from magic squares, but he shows no interest whatsoever.

You can use the formula explained in this book to create magic squares as well as yantras. Instead of using someone's date of birth, you can simply place any four numbers in the top row, and create a magic square that will impress others. However, this will not be a yantra as it is not related to anyone or anything. It becomes a yantra only when you use the specific numbers from a person's date of birth, as it then relates to them personally.

Because of the special properties of magic squares, they

have been used as lucky charms and talismans for thousands of years. If you want to attract love, for example, it is possible to draw up a special magic square, based on your date of birth, that will help bring the right relationship to you. Do you want more money? It is a simple matter to construct a magic square, again based on your date of birth, that will attract money.

For thousands of years people have carried their own, special number squares around with them, for protection and good luck. By using these number squares you will be taking part in an ancient tradition that is as relevant today as it ever has been in the past. Many people think that you need to be good at math to construct magic squares. Fortunately, this is not the case for the number squares in this book. Although they appear mysterious and complex, they are in fact extremely easy to do. However, I seldom let on to others just how simple they are to construct as I enjoy the comments people make after I have drawn up a number square for them. They think that I must be a genius at math, when all I have done is some simple addition and subtraction.

The first magic square was found in the markings of a tortoise shell some 5,000 years ago in China. It is shown in Figure 3A on page 20. The story goes that a young man called Wu was making improvements to the Yellow River to try to stop the flooding that frequently destroyed the fertile plains. While he and his men were working on the river, a large tortoise crawled out. This was considered a good omen, as in those days the people believed that gods lived inside the shells of turtles and tortoises. When Wu discovered the strange markings on the shell he summoned

16	3	2	13
5	10	11	8
9	6	7	12
4	15	14	1

*Figure Introduction A: the Magic Square
from Dürer's* Melancholy *of 1514*

all the wise men to come and examine it. From their study came the I Ching, feng shui, Chinese astrology and Chinese numerology. Partly because of this discovery, Wu of Hsia became the first emperor of China.

Magic squares quickly spread around the world. The early Hebrew kabbalists thought that the 3 x 3 magic square represented the forbidden name of God. Later on, alchemists believed that the 3 x 3 magic square held the secret of turning base metals into gold.

In the Middle Ages magic squares were commonly engraved on silver and worn as lucky talismans. During the Great Plague in Europe they became even more popular as

52	61	4	13	20	29	36	45
14	3	62	51	46	35	30	19
53	60	5	12	21	28	37	44
11	6	59	54	43	38	27	22
55	58	7	10	23	26	39	42
9	8	57	56	41	40	25	24
50	63	2	15	18	31	34	47
16	1	64	49	48	33	32	17

Figure Introduction B

they were believed to be a protection from disease.

Probably the most famous magic square of all is the one that appears in Albrecht Durer's famous woodcut, *Melancholy*. This 4 x 4 magic square contains the year it was created (1514) in the two central squares on the bottom row (see Figure Introduction A). This magic square was probably included in the woodcut as astrologers of that time believed that magic squares could cure people suffering from melancholy.

Naturally, mathematicians have always been fascinated with magic squares. Benjamin Franklin, in his autobiography, tells of his interest in them. In his youth he spent countless hours working out ways to construct elaborate magic squares. Many years later, a friend showed him a book on magic squares written by a French mathematician. In this book the Frenchman commented that English-speaking people were not as good as the French in creating magic squares. Benjamin Franklin went away and returned the next day with an 8 x 8 magic square he had devised (see Figure Introduction B). His friend then showed him another book which included a 16 x 16 magic square. He said that constructing a square like this would "be a work of great labour." Benjamin Franklin went away again and returned the following day with a 16 x 16 magic square that contained many more properties than the one in his friend's book.

I have included a little bit of the history of magic squares so that you can see how they have captivated and helped people throughout history. I am sure that you will find them just as fascinating. More importantly, though, you will be able to construct number squares for yourself and your friends and use them for love, luck and protection.

chapter one

YANTRAS

All yantras are mandalas. A mandala is usually a circular design drawn around a central point that symbolizes the universe. In India there are two types of mandalas that are known as yantras: pictorial yantras and magic-square yantras.

PICTORIAL YANTRAS

A pictorial yantra is a symbolic diagram, usually used for meditation purposes. It is a geometrical form creating a complex mandala. The word *yantra* comes from the Sanskrit. *Yam* means to support and *Trana* means freedom from bondage. Consequently, a yantra frees and supports. Yantras are designed to allow you to withdraw into yourself and become aware of the divine being within. In the East, they have always known the truth of Christ's words:

1

"Behold, the kingdom of God is within you" (Luke XVII, 21). In effect, yantras are symbolic pictures of the divine and need to be treated with reverence. There are believed to be 960 pictorial yantras.[1]

Interior decorators in the West frequently use yantras as decorations and are completely unaware of what they really are. They would think twice about using the Christian cross as a mere decoration, but have no hesitation in using symbols from other religions as wall hangings. In fact, a yantra is, perhaps, even more spiritual than a Christian cross, as it is believed that God lives inside every yantra.

All pictorial yantras have a dot or small circle at the center. This is known as the *bindu* and is the focal point for meditation. In fact, even a simple dot can be regarded as a yantra, as it contains the One inside it. A dot is complete in itself and signifies God. A quote from the *Upanishads* expresses this perfectly: "God, being the immovable mover, the One behind all events in the cosmos, is the still point around which everything revolves." When people meditate on a pictorial yantra they become one with the yantra in the *bindu*. In effect they are becoming one with God. In meditation the *bindu* and the sixth chakra, known as the "third eye," are joined as one.

Frequently, a mantra is said when meditating on a yantra. *Om* is the best known mantra in the West, but there are countless others used for different purposes. Mantras are sacred words taken from the ancient Vedic scriptures. You might think that mantras work because of the belief of the person chanting them. In fact, mantras work because the vibrations of the sounds on the nervous system cause beneficial effects on the person reciting them.[2]

The dot is the center of the yantra. It relates to the spirit. Around this are placed different geometrical figures: circles, triangles, squares, and lotuses. In meditation, all of these lead you to the center.

The circle derives from the movement of the planets and is a symbol of wholeness and totality. It relates to air.

The triangle symbolizes the three worlds of Sattva, Rajas, and Tamas, or neutral, positive, and negative. It relates to fire. When the apex points downward, the triangle is a symbol of the yoni and represents feminine energy. When the triangle is pointing upward, it represents male energy. Often, the two triangles are represented as a five-pointed star, and this symbolizes the five elements of earth, water, air, energy, and space.

The square symbolizes earth and the material world. The four gates or openings in the sides represent the baser instincts that have to be overcome before one can merge completely with the yantra.

Mandalas traditionally use circles and squares. The circle symbolizes the cosmos, and the square, the Earth. This corresponds to the yang and the yin of the *I Ching*. The yang is male, celestial, and pioneering, while the yin is the female, nurturing, earth.

The lotus is a symbol of purity. In a yantra it represents the unfolding of oneself and the expanding of one's consciousness. Lotus plants begin their life in the mud and gradually grow to rest triumphantly on the surface of the water, pure and perfect. Lotus petals are also symbolized in the chakras, each petal representing the unfolding and development of a specific quality. The ultimate is the *Sahasrara Chakra*, a thousand-petalled lotus above the head.[3]

Figure 1A: the Shri Yantra

The most complex and best known of the pictorial yantras is also one of the oldest. This is the Shri Yantra (see Figure 1A). This yantra combines elements of Shiva and Shakti, who together comprise the cosmos. In fact, the Shri Yantra is sometimes called the Yantra of the Cosmos. Because the design of this yantra is so complex, with its intersection of nine triangles, contemplation of it should be done only in daylight.

There are two versions of the Shri Yantra. One has five upward-pointing triangles and four downward. The other reverses this with four upward-pointing and five downward.

Most yantras are symmetrical and balanced. The Shri
Yantra would conform to this if it contained four upward
and four downward-pointing triangles. The additional
triangle adds strength and power to the yantra. Interestingly enough, the yantra still looks symmetrical.

The Shri Yantra represents all nine chakras, surrounded by two rings of lotus petals which create a
mandala of the Moon.

ASTROLOGICAL YANTRAS

Astrological yantras are used when the energies of the nine
planets are required. This is usually when a certain planet
is afflicted in a person's natal chart. It is believed that if the
person wears the specific yantra for the planet, the defect
will be overcome, or at least minimized. The planets are:
Sun, Moon, Mercury, Venus, Mars, Jupiter, and Saturn,
plus the two nodes of the Moon. The North Node is
known as *Rahu,* or the Dragon's Head, and the South Node
is *Ketu,* or the Dragon's Tail.

The Sun yantra is believed to eliminate the negative
aspects of an afflicted Sun and to give peace of mind. This
yantra should be engraved on copper or stainless steel and
worn around the neck. It can also be drawn on paper and
carried in a purse or in a pocket. The best time to construct
it is on a Sunday. Each row adds up to 111, and the grand
total of all the numbers is 666 (see Figure 1B).

There are mantras designed for each astrological
yantra. Each mantra has to be chanted a certain number of
times. To assist with this, strings of beads, similar to rosary
beads, are used. Each string consists of 108 beads. One
bead, known as the Guru bead, is slightly larger than the

1	35	3	34	32	6
30	8	28	27	11	7
13	23	22	21	14	18
24	17	16	15	20	19
14	26	9	10	29	25
31	2	33	4	5	36

Figure 1B: Sun Yantra

others and tells the person using it when he or she has chanted the mantra 108 times. At this stage, the person either stops, or goes back the other way, so that the Guru bead is never crossed.[4]

The Moon yantra should be engraved on silver or written on white paper, and kept on the person. It is used when the Moon is afflicted in the person's chart and gives the wearer good friends and respect in the community. It should be drawn on a Monday. It is a 9 x 9 magic square. Each row adds up to 369, and the grand total is 3321.

1	15	14	4
12	6	7	9
8	10	11	5
13	3	2	16

Figure 1C: Jupiter Yantra

4	9	2
3	5	7
8	1	6

Figure 1D: Saturn Yantra

The Mercury yantra is an 8 x 8 magic square that totals 3180. It should be engraved on a silver plate or drawn on paper on a Wednesday. It protects the wearer from enemies and increases memory retention.

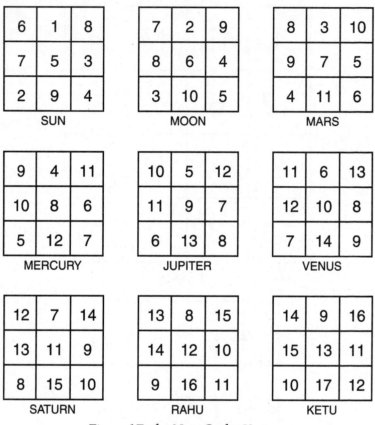

Figure 1E: the Nav-Graha Yantras

The Venus yantra is a 7 x 7 magic square that enhances peace of mind and makes one more attractive to the opposite sex. It should be constructed on a Friday, and can be made from any material.

The Mars yantra should be written on a copper plate on a Tuesday. It is a 5 x 5 magic square that totals 325. It protects the wearer from accidents and other injury.

The Jupiter yantra is a standard 4 x 4 magic square utilizing all the numbers from one to sixteen (see Figure 1C). Each row adds up to 34, and the grand total of all the numbers is 136. It can be made from any metal or paper, but should be drawn on a Tuesday, or when Jupiter and the Moon are in a trine aspect. It gives the wearer power, prestige, and authority.

The Saturn yantra is a variant of the standard 3 x 3 magic square (see Figure 1D). It should be engraved on copper, or drawn on paper or parchment. It gives the opportunity to attain worldly success. It is also believed to be helpful in curing depression.

There is also a range of 3 x 3 yantras that are specifically designed to prevent the ill effects of malefic planets, either in the birth chart, or in transits (see Figure 1E). These are called the Nav-Graha, or nine-planet, yantras.

NUMEROLOGICAL YANTRAS

These are the yantras that we are primarily concerned with in this book. They are worn as talismans to provide protection and attract good things to the wearer. They are also used for divination purposes. Most of them are magic squares.

MAGIC SQUARES

M agic squares have intrigued mathematicians and occultists for thousands of years. Mathematicians find their perfection a source of beauty and have worked out many ways of creating them.

ODD-NUMBERED SQUARES

The simplest possible magic square is constructed on a 3 x 3 grid (see Figure 2A).

To construct it, all we need do is put the first number (a 1) in the middle of the top row. We then move diagonally upward to the right. This would necessitate the number 2 being placed above the top right-hand square. As there is no square in that position, we move to the very bottom of that column and put the number 2 in the bottom

8	1	6
3	5	7
4	9	2

Figure 2A

right-hand square. Again, we have a problem as there is no place to insert the number 3 diagonally up from number 2. Consequently, we go to the far left-hand side of that row and insert the number 3 in that position. Again, we see that we can not insert number 4 diagonally up from number 3 as number 1 is already in that position. In this case, we insert the number 4 right below number 3. Now we can insert number 5 diagonally up from number 4 in the center of the magic square. Number 6 is placed in position, diagonally up from number 5. Number 7 has to go diagonally up from number 6. As there is no square there, it would normally go in the square that number 4 is in. As the square is taken, number 7 is placed immediately below number 6. If we move diagonally up from number 7, we again find ourselves outside the magic square, so we go to the far left-hand side of that row and insert number 8 in the top left-hand corner. There is only one empty space now. We move diagonally up from number 8 and, finding that it takes us outside the magic square, drop to the bottom of the column and insert number 9 in the last position.

17	24	1	8	15
23	5	7	14	16
4	6	13	20	22
10	12	19	21	3
11	18	25	2	9

Figure 2B

It has taken a large amount of room to describe this, but in practice it is very simple. All you do is move up and diagonally to the right. It is easier to understand if you picture the magic square as a tube with the top and bottom rows joined. It is also a tube the other way with the left and right hand columns joined as well.

Let's try it again with a 5 x 5 magic square (see Figure 2B). Again, we start with the number 1 in the middle of the top row. Imagine that the top and bottom rows are joined, creating a tube. Number 2 goes diagonally up and to the right of number 1. This places it in the fourth square from the left in the bottom row. Number 3 fits in nicely up and to the right of number 2. Now we have to imagine that the left- and right-hand sides are also joined, making another tube. Number 4 goes into position diagonally up and to the right of number 3. This places it in the third square from the top in the left-hand column. Number 5 goes into place easily, but number 1 is already in the square that should hold number 6. Consequently, number 6 is placed in the square immediately below number 5. Numbers 7 and 8 fit in naturally on the diagonal, as does number 9 if you imagine the magic square as a tube.

The rest of the magic square is built in exactly the same way. It is much easier than it looks, and after doing a few, I am sure you could impress your high school math teacher with what you can do!

I have included a picture of a 7 x 7 magic square (see Figure 2C). See if you can construct it by yourself before looking at the illustration. If you get carried away, you might want to construct a 9 x 9, or perhaps a 37 x 37 magic square!

The rules for constructing odd-numbered magic squares are very straightforward:

1. Place the number 1 in the center of the top row.
2. Number 2 goes diagonally up and to the right. As there is no box there, you must imagine the square as a tube, and place it in the bottom box in the next row.
3. Continue going diagonally upwards in a right-hand direction until you come to a box that already has a number in it. When this occurs, place the next number in the box immediately below the last number.
4. Keep on until all the squares are filled.

30	39	48	1	10	19	28
38	47	7	9	18	27	29
46	6	8	17	26	35	37
5	14	16	25	34	36	45
13	15	24	33	42	44	4
21	23	32	41	43	3	12
22	31	40	49	2	11	20

Figure 2C

You can also experiment by moving up diagonally to the left, rather than the right. This works just as well. If you play chess you will be familiar with the move of the knight —two up and one across, or one up and two across. You can make interesting magic squares with this move. Ensure though, that if you decide on, say, two up and one to the right, that you stay with this move throughout the magic square. It will not work if at some point in the construction you start doing one up and two to the right, or two up and one to the left.

1	2	3	4
5	6	7	8
9	10	11	12
13	14	15	16

Figure 2D

EVEN-NUMBERED SQUARES

Even numbered squares are harder to construct than the odd ones. There are many methods of making them, and in Chapter Four we'll learn the correct method of constructing yantra magic squares. In the meantime, here is an interesting way to create a 4 x 4 magic square.

Start by writing the number 1 in the top left-hand box. Number 2 goes in the next box, followed by numbers 3 and 4. That completes the top row. The next row contains numbers 5, 6, 7, and 8. Continue in this fashion until the numbers from 1 to 16 are all in sequence (see Figure 2D).

Now we need to remove the two middle numbers in all of the outside rows. This means numbers 2 and 3 in the top row are removed, as are numbers 14 and 15 in the bottom row. Finally, numbers 5 and 9 are removed from

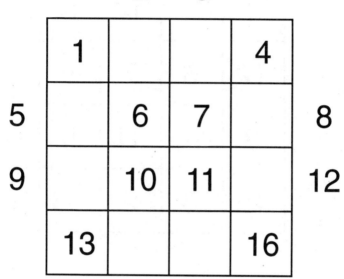

Figure 2E

the left-hand-side vertical row, and numbers 8 and 12 from the right-hand side (see Figure 2E).

These numbers are now replaced in an interesting manner. Numbers 2 and 3 are reversed and placed in the positions vacated by numbers 14 and 15. This means the new bottom row reads: 13, 3, 2, and 16. Likewise, the numbers 14 and 15 are reversed and placed in the positions originally belonging to numbers 2 and 3. The new top row now reads: 1, 15, 14, and 4. You can imagine what happens next. The numbers 8 and 12 are reversed and inserted where numbers 5 and 9 were. Finally, the

1	15	14	4
12	6	7	9
8	10	11	5
13	3	2	16

Figure 2F

numbers 5 and 9 are reversed and placed in the two positions on the right-hand, vertical side (see Figure 2F).

You will find this magic square adds up to 34 in every direction.

You can create any size 4 x 4 magic square in this manner providing the sixteen numbers are in series. If you construct a magic square that goes 3, 6, 9, 12, etc. you will find that it totals 102 in every direction.

There are many other methods of constructing even-numbered magic squares.[1] Some methods are highly complex and are of interest only to mathematicians. Fortunately, the method of creating yantra magic squares based on the date of birth is extremely easy.

chapter three

THE AMAZING SQUARE OF WU

When Wu of Hsia[1] uncovered the tortoise while making improvements to the Hwang Ho (Yellow) River to prevent flooding, he had little idea of the dramatic effect it would have on the divination systems of the world.

At this time the Chinese believed that God lived in tortoise shells and water buffalo horns, so Wu was delighted to find it. Especially so, as the tortoise was also regarded as an indicator of longevity and happiness.

Wu was astonished to find what appeared to be a perfect magic square in the markings of the tortoise's shell (see Figure 3A). This is known as the *Lo Shu,* or River Picture. He regarded this as being a message from God that would help him rule his country in such a way that everyone would be happy and enjoy long, productive lives.

4	9	2
3	5	7
8	1	6

Figure 3A

Chinese civilization was well advanced in the time of Wu (2953–2838 B.C.).[2] They had a written language and a complex system of religious beliefs that emphasized ancestor worship and general respect for the past.

They also had a divination system that used "oracle bones." The oracle bones were usually made from the shoulder blade of an ox or the plastron (bottom shell) of a tortoise. Questions were engraved on the surface and then heat was applied, causing the bones to crack. The designs that appeared as a result of this were then interpreted.

Heating of bones had been known since the end of the fifth millennium B.C. when Neolithic farmers began the practice. As their written language contained few characters at that time, only simple questions could be asked. It is believed that they interpreted the cracks in heated bones after stating their questions out loud. By the time of Wu, very complex questions were being engraved on the bones and many of these still survive. They have proved invaluable in researching the Chinese written languages. At the time of Wu there were at least 4,000 characters and the questions used five of our seven parts of speech (pronouns, verbs, adverbs, adjectives, and prepositions).

Almost all of the bones that have been recovered were used for divination, but a small number were used to record the Shang calendar and to record tribute payments. The Shang calendar was a lunar one, based on six weeks, each ten days long. The cycle of sixty is still used in China today.

Probably the largest collection of oracle bones outside China is stored in the Carnegie Institute Museum in Pittsburgh.[3]

The design on Wu's tortoise formed a perfect 3 x 3 magic square (see Figure 3A). Each row adds up to fifteen, horizontally, vertically, and diagonally. Over time this square formed the basis of the *I Ching,* Chinese astrology, *feng-shui,* the *ki,* Japanese *Kigaku,* and other forms of numerology.

The markings on the tortoise were black and white. Black was attributed to yin and white to yang. Apparently, the odd numbers were white and the even numbers black. The Chinese Taoists regarded the whole universe as being classified into yin or yang. They moved slightly away from Wu's original findings when they decided which of the nine numbers were lucky and which were unlucky. One, three, and eight symbolized good luck to the Taoists. Five could be either good or bad luck. Two, four, six, seven, and nine all symbolized bad luck.[4]

The ancient tradition states that the tortoise shell was kept at the court of the emperor until 1079 B.C. when it was lost. In the twelfth century A.D. a copy was produced, but it is not known how true to the original it is. Some writers have taken exception to the use of this twelfth

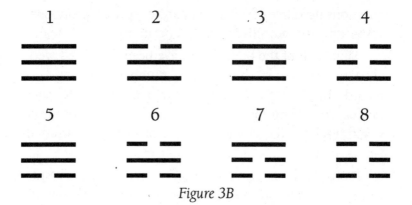

Figure 3B

century reproduction by modern authors.[5] Confucius mentioned the tortoise shell in his *Analects* when he wrote "The river gives forth no more diagrams."[6]

Wu's magic square quickly spread around the world. Pythagoras and his followers studied it. In medieval times Cornelius Agrippa named it the Square of Saturn, and many believed that it held the secret of alchemy.

THE I CHING

Wu of Hsia derived the original eight trigrams of the *I Ching* from the magic square on the turtle's back. Some authorities claim that this occurred in 3322 B.C.[7] The long, unbroken lines represent yang energy, and the broken lines, yin. The eight original trigrams (known as *Pa Kua*) were not named or explained, as this was not necessary for people who were used to deciphering pictures (see Figure 3B).

By about 2205 B.C. the trigrams had been multiplied to form the 64 hexagrams. About 1150 B.C. King Wan became the first person to record the meanings of all of the hexagrams. As he was in prison at the time, he had to be very careful with what he wrote, and much of it was deliberately obscure. Two years later, his son, Due of Kau, wrote a more open version of the meanings. Most modern translations rely on his work.

THE T'AI HSÜAN CHING

Another ancient Chinese system of divination, the *T'ai Hsüan Ching,* is also derived from Wu's magic square but has evolved to use nine 9 x 9 magic squares. All of the numbers from 1 to 729 are used only once. When placed on top of each other to form a cube, these diagrams create additional magic squares horizontally, vertically, and diagonally. Each column of this cube adds up to 3285. The number in the middle box of the center magic square, when they are all placed on top of each other, is 365, the number of days in the year. The whole system of *T'ai Hsüan Ching* revolves around this center, creating a work of incredible beauty, mathematical perfection, and numerological wholeness.[8] The *T'ai Hsüan Ching* is used primarily for divination and answers can be found using astrology, numerology, or by tossing stalks of milfoil.

THE KI

The ancient Chinese divination system known as the *ki* uses the yin and yang (the black and white), but also uses the basic magic square (see Figure 3A).

However, in this system the numbers move around to create eight other squares (see Figure 3C). These are not "magic" squares as the numbers do not add up to 15. The number that is placed in the center box of the square is determined by the year in which you were born. You can

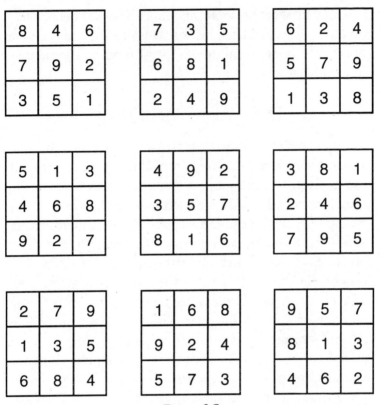

Figure 3C

determine this number from Figure 3D. (Bear in mind when looking at this chart that in *ki* the year starts on February 3 and continues to February 2 of the following year. If you were born in January 1960, the center number of your chart would be five, not four, as you would be classed as being born in 1959.) Your particular square can then be interpreted as each box contains a house of experience (see Figure 3E).

Year	Number	Year	Number	Year	Number	Year	Number
1901	9	1931	6	1961	3	1991	9
1902	8	1932	5	1962	2	1992	8
1903	7	1933	4	1963	1	1993	7
1904	6	1934	3	1964	9	1994	6
1905	5	1935	2	1965	8	1995	5
1906	4	1936	1	1966	7	1996	4
1907	3	1937	9	1967	6	1997	3
1908	2	1938	8	1968	5	1998	2
1909	1	1939	7	1969	4	1999	1
1910	9	1940	6	1970	3	2000	9
1911	8	1941	5	1971	2	2001	8
1912	7	1942	4	1972	1	2002	7
1913	6	1943	3	1973	9	2003	6
1914	5	1944	2	1974	8	2004	5
1915	4	1945	1	1975	7	2005	4
1916	3	1946	9	1976	6	2006	3
1917	2	1947	8	1977	5	2007	2
1918	1	1948	7	1978	4	2008	1
1919	9	1949	6	1979	3	2009	9
1920	8	1950	5	1980	2	2010	8
1921	7	1951	4	1981	1	2011	7
1922	6	1952	3	1982	9	2012	6
1923	5	1953	2	1983	8	2013	5
1924	4	1954	1	1984	7	2014	4
1925	3	1955	9	1985	6	2015	3
1926	2	1956	8	1986	5	2016	2
1927	1	1957	7	1987	4	2017	1
1928	9	1958	6	1988	3	2018	9
1929	8	1959	5	1989	2	2019	8
1930	7	1960	4	1990	1	2020	7

Figure 3D

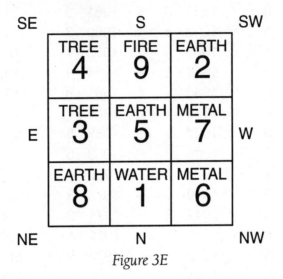

Figure 3E

One — White Water

People born with number one in the center of their chart are easy-going, adaptable, and often engage in creative activities. They are good listeners who empathize well with others. They possess good judgment and frequently rise to positions of great responsibility. They are natural leaders.

Two — Black Earth

People born with number two in the center of their charts are stable, thoughtful, and sociable. They are honest and sincere but also rather sensitive. They enjoy paying attention to the details and sometimes miss the whole picture. As they find it hard to delegate, they usually prefer to work by themselves.

Three — Turquoise Tree

People born with number three in the center of their charts are curious and impulsive. They express their views clearly and find it hard to hold back their feelings. They are romantic, idealistic, and easily hurt. They have quick, astute brains that often enable them to achieve considerable financial success.

Four — Green Tree

The number four tree is more thoughtful and considerate than the number three. People born with the number four in the central position have good intellects and make excellent philosophers and administrators. They are honest and react strongly when they feel that justice is not being done. They are often better with the overall view, rather than the details.

Five — Yellow Earth

People with the number five in the center of the chart have the magic square that Wu discovered as their chart. These people are realistic, practical, and down-to-earth. They are sound thinkers and frequently attract others to them with their good common sense. They appear gentle on the outside, but can stand up for themselves when necessary. They enjoy learning for the sheer joy of it. They enjoy challenges that are worthy of their abilities.

Six — White Metal

People born with a six in the center of their chart are strong-willed and usually show little of what they are really thinking inside. They keep their thoughts to themselves. They are also self-contained and frequently find it hard to establish and maintain friendships. Although they often appear proud, they have an insecure side to their natures.

Seven — Red Metal

People born with a seven in the center of their charts are practical and keep their feet firmly on the ground. They are good at dealing with others and make excellent diplomats and peacemakers. They enjoy luxury and, when possible, surround themselves with attractive possessions and clothing. Their communication skills are excellent and they usually choose a career where these talents can be utilized.

Eight — White Earth

People with an eight at the center of their charts are serious, refined, and intelligent. They think before speaking, and are usually introspective in nature. They are cautious and like to test the waters before starting anything new. They often achieve success in later life. Many of these people are adventurous and develop a taste for travel.

Nine — Purple Fire

People with a nine in the center of their charts are outgoing, adventurous, and sociable. They are good at dealing with the public, and at anticipating the public's needs. They can be impulsive and speak too quickly on occasion. Consequently, they prefer to make friends with people who have similar views to their own. They are usually successful in business, knowing how to get on with their customers and how to buy and sell at the right price.

The *ki* system is extremely useful in determining compatibility. The five elements (fire, earth, water, metal, and wood [or tree]) either help or hurt each other. For example, if water is placed on wood, it helps it to grow. However, water does not help a fire, as it puts it out. Consequently,

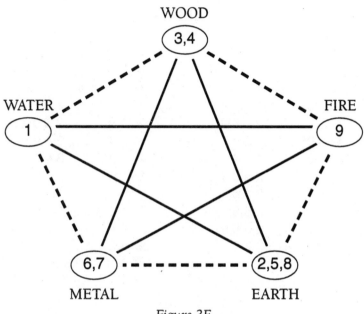

Figure 3F

someone born in White Water would not get on well with someone born in Purple Fire. But the person born in White Water would get on well with someone born in Green Tree.

The system is illustrated in Figure 3F. The numbers in the circles around the outside get on well with the numbers in the circles on either side of them (following the dotted lines), but do not harmonize with the numbers diagonally across.

The best combinations for compatibility are shown in Figure 3G.

The *ki* system of astrology and numerology is highly complex. What we have looked at here is a mere glimpse, similar to a quick glance at the twelve Sun signs of Western astrology.

COMPATIBILITY TABLE

For Men			For Women		
Natal Year	Best Partner	Favorable Partner	Natal Year	Best Partner	Favorable Partner
1	3,4	1,6,7	1	6,7	1,3,4
2	6,7	2,5,8,9	2	9	2,5,6,7,8
3	9	1,3,4	3	1	3,4,9
4	9	1,3,4	4	1	3,4,9
5	6,7	2,5,8,9	5	9	2,5,6,7,8
6	1	2,5,6,7,8	6	2,5,8	1,6,7
7	1	2,5,6,7,8	7	2,5,8	1,6,7
8	6,7	2,5,8,9	8	9	2,5,6,7,8
9	2,5,8	3,4,9	9	3,4	2,5,8,9

Figure 3G

FENG-SHUI

Feng-shui means "wind and water" and is a system of living in harmony with the laws of nature. It derives from the yin and the yang, and is consequently related to Wu's tortoise.

The nine boxes in Wu's magic square are regarded as being the nine palaces of the Ming T'ang, the temple that the Emperor lived in. As the seasons of the year changed, he would move from room to room in the temple.

In spring the Emperor would live for a month at a time in each of the three rooms of the Ch'ing Yang (Green Yang) Palace. This was in the east part of the imperial residence. In the summer he would live for three months in the red south part, again spending one month in each room. He would then spend a short period of time in the yellow center of the imperial palace. It is not known how long this period lasted. Following this, he would spend fall in the white west part of his residence, and complete the year by spending winter in the three rooms of the black north.[9] As you can see, the Emperor's palace symbolized the magic square of Wu.

Consequently, the nine boxes of Wu's square indicate the best rooms in the house for certain activities, and as bedrooms for different members of the family.

Remember that in this square south is shown at the top. The following shows the best rooms for the family:[10]

South	Father
North	Mother
Southwest	Eldest son
East	Middle son
Northwest	Youngest son
Northeast	Eldest daughter
West	Middle daughter
Southeast	Youngest daughter

However, most of the system of *feng-shui* used today dates only from the time of the Sung dynasty (1126–1278 A.D.). The tenets of *feng-shui* state that in the beginning there was "absolute nothing." When this "absolute nothing" first moved it created the male. After a while it rested, and while resting, produced the female. Here we have the yin and the yang. After it had completed resting, it moved again, and has continued to move and rest ever since. The male and female can also be interpreted as heaven and earth. By a system of constant growth and change all of the elements of the world came into being. The male and female energies continue to intermingle, sometimes harmonizing, sometimes aggravating each other. *Ki* is the name for the life-force, or energy, that keeps everything moving.

PLANES OF PYTHAGORAS

The magic square of Wu is still being used to create new divination systems today. The system often known as the Planes of Pythagoras appears to have been invented separately by a number of people over the last hundred years. Austin Coates, a celebrated orientalist, is just one person who developed this system independently after forty years of study.[11] The earliest book I have been able to find on this system of numerology is *Numbers and Their Influence*, published in 1940.[12] Hettie Templeton, the author of this book, lived in Australia and it is because of her insight and considerable skills as a teacher that this system of numerology is better known in Australasia than anywhere else. In recent years several Australian authors have written books on this system of numerology.

The Planes of Pythagoras method uses the 3 x 3 grid, but the numbers from a person's date of birth are entered in a special way (see Figure 3H). All the "1s" are placed in the lower left-side box. Someone born on July 17, 1965, would have two 1s in that box. One of these comes from the 17 (1+7) and the other from the 1965 (1+9+6+5). This person would also have two 7s in the lower right-hand box, one 5 in the center box, one 6 in the top middle box, and one 9 in the top right-hand box. The completed chart is shown in Figure 3I.

Once the numbers are in position we look for any "arrows." This system is sometimes known as the "Arrows of Pythagoras" as he used a system of sixteen directional

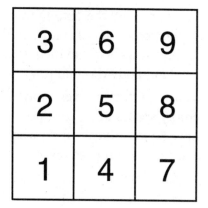

Figure 3H

	6	9
	5	
11		77

Figure 3I

arrows to interpret charts.[13] The arrows are created if the chart has any vertical, horizontal, or diagonal rows that have either a number in every box, or no numbers in any box. The chart we are looking at has one arrow: the numbers 1, 5, and 9 create a diagonal arrow.

Each level, or plane, of the chart represents different areas of the person's life. The top row (numbers 3, 6, and 9) represents the intellect, the middle row (2, 5, and 8) represents the emotions, and the bottom row (1, 4, and 7) represents the practical side of life. Another way of describing these three rows is to call them mind (top row), soul (middle row), and body (bottom row).

Someone who is perfect in every way would have a chart with no empty spaces in it. This, not surprisingly, is impossible. Empty boxes indicate areas where the person needs to work hard to learn the lesson of the box.

Each number has a meaning:

One

This is the number of self-expression. People with just one 1 in their chart find it hard to express what they really feel. People with two 1s have the ability to express themselves easily, and can see both sides of an argument. People with three 1s are often "chatterboxes," though you can find very quiet people with three 1s as well. Sometimes, both sides can be found in the same person. People with four or more 1s find it very hard to express themselves.

Two

This is the number of intuition and sensitivity. People with one 2 are naturally intuitive, but easily hurt. More than one 2 accentuates this.

Three

This number strengthens the imagination and heightens the intellect. One or two 3s is regarded as positive, but people with more 3s than this tend to lead their lives in a world of their own making.

Four

This is the number of practicality and hard work. People with a 4 in their chart are prepared to work hard for what they get. People with two or more 4s work well with their hands, but find it hard to progress in life.

Five

This number gives emotional stability and the ability to understand and empathize easily with others. People with two or more 5s need to pay particular attention to their home and family life, as this is where they are likely to have the greatest difficulty.

Six

This is the number of home and family. People with one 6 will be happiest at home, surrounded by loved ones. If they do not have a home of their own, they will become very involved with someone who does. People with two or more 6s are inclined to worry about their home and family.

Seven

Seven is the number of sacrifice. People with a 7 in their chart have to learn the hard way, usually through a loss or disappointment. The more 7s in the chart, the more this is emphasized.

Eight

This is the number of logic and attention to detail. People with two or more 8s also have this quality, but tend to be restless and move around a great deal.

Nine

This is the number of idealism. Everyone born this century has at least one 9, marking a period where humanity becomes more aware of the needs of others. People with two 9s are deep thinkers. They can be critical of people less intelligent than they are. People with three or more 9s have a large weighting of numbers on the mental plane and need to learn to relax and take things calmly.

Now we can look at the arrows.

Arrow of the Intellect (3, 6, and 9)

This arrow gives a good brain, and emphasizes the intellect ahead of feelings. People with this arrow need constant mental stimulation.

Arrow of Emotional Balance (2, 5, and 8)

This arrow effectively balances the spiritual and physical sides of life, giving people with it a natural emotional balance.

Arrow of Practicality (1, 4, and 7)

This arrow gives a practical, physical, and often material-istic approach to life. People with it are good with their hands, but this can take many forms: plumbers as well as concert pianists, for instance, could have this arrow.

Arrow of the Planner (1, 2, and 3)

This arrow gives a love of order, and combines thought, intuition, and self-expression. People with it enjoy plan-ning ahead.

Arrow of Will Power (4, 5, and 6)

This arrow belongs to people who are so intent on achieving their own desires that they can be oblivious to the needs of others.

Arrow of Activity (7, 8, and 9)

People with this arrow like to express themselves with action. They also need peace and quiet as there is often an overabundance of nervous energy.

Arrow of Determination (1, 5, and 9)

This arrow gives great determination, coupled with persistence and patience.

Arrow of Spirituality (3, 5, and 7)

This arrow gives an inner serenity and a deep spiritual awareness.

Arrow of Poor Memory (Spaces in 3, 6, and 9)

It is impossible for anyone born this century to have this arrow, but it will occur again shortly. People with this gradually become more forgetful as they get older.

Arrow of Hypersensitivity (Spaces in 2, 5, and 8)

People with this are often shy and can be easily hurt. They are also very sensitive.

Arrow of Frustrations (Spaces in 4, 5, and 6)

People with this expect more from others than they are prepared to give. They suffer many setbacks and frustrations.

Arrow of Skepticism (Spaces in 3, 5, and 7)

People with this arrow develop a questioning type of faith as they progress through life. Many professional psychics have this arrow.

Let's interpret the chart of the person born on July 17, 1965 (see Figure 31). We could say to this person:

"You are a caring person. You enjoy helping people and are always ready to lend a hand when required. (This information comes from the Life Path which is discussed in Chapter Seven.)

"You have one arrow in your chart—the Arrow of Determination. This is good, as it means you can hang in there when things get tough. You are persistent and patient.

"On the mental level you have a 6 and a 9. This gives you a good brain, but a specialized one. If something interests you, you can pick it up very quickly. If it doesn't, you might as well forget it. The 6 means that you are a family-minded person. You enjoy being home with your loved ones around you. It emphasizes your humanitarian qualities.

"The 5 on the emotional plane is a good number. It gives you emotional stability and the ability to understand and empathize with others. It is the pivot point of the chart, whichever way you look at it.

"On the practical level you have two 7s and two 1s. Seven means learning the hard way, often through a loss or disappointment. Things often go wrong before they come right. Basically, you learn from your mistakes.

"Two 1s is perfect, as it give you the ability to express yourself easily and get along well with others. You can easily see other people's point of view."

Isn't the depth of information amazing, even with just a quick glance at this system of numerology? It is possible to glean much more information from this chart by examining areas we have not even mentioned, such as the missing numbers. Such things are outside the scope of this book, but there are many excellent books available on this system of numerology. (See "Bibliography and Suggested Reading" at the back of the book.)

I find it endlessly fascinating that the 3 x 3 square found by Wu of Hsia has been interpreted in a variety of ways to create many other systems that are still able to help people thousands of years after its discovery. It is also intriguing to speculate on the effect this square has had on the development of computers. Gottfried Leibnitz, the inventor of the binary system, was an enthusiastic student of the *I Ching*.[14]

chapter four

YOUR PERSONAL YANTRA

Your personal yantra is a magic square based on your date of birth. It can be interpreted to provide amazing insights into your character and motivations.

The top row of your personal yantra is created from your date of birth. This is entered into a 4 x 4 magic square with each of the sixteen small boxes labeled with a letter of the alphabet. The first box in the top left-hand corner would be labeled "A," the one next to it "B," and so on, ending up with the letter "P" in the lower right-hand corner box.

For the sake of example, we'll use an imaginary person born on August 14, 1965. Let's call her Crystal.

We put the number of the month Crystal was born in in Box A. Being born in August, the eighth month, we place "8" in Box A. Next we put the day of birth in Box B.

This is "14." In Box C we place the last two digits of the year in which Crystal was born. As she was born in 1965, we place "65" in Box C.

So far we have filled up the first three squares in the top row. The final box ("D") is obtained by adding up all the numbers in Crystal's entire date of birth and bringing them down to a single digit. There is one exception to this. If at any stage in bringing the numbers down to a single digit we encounter either an 11 or 22, we stop reducing at that point. Eleven and 22 are called Master Numbers and we will go into the meanings of these in the next chapter.

We also add up the numbers of the date of birth by creating a sum, rather than by adding them up in a straight line. Consequently, we add up Crystal's date of birth like this:

$$8$$
$$14$$
$$\underline{1965}$$
$$1987 = 1+9+8+7 = 25, \text{ and } 2+5 = 7.$$

We place "7" in Box D. This completes the first row of Crystal's magic square, or yantra (see Figure 4A).

Let's do another one. A good friend of mine was born on February 29, 1944.

$$2$$
$$29$$
$$\underline{1944}$$
$$1975, = 1+9+7+5 = 22.$$

Remember what I said about 11 and 22? My friend would put 22 in Box D, as neither 11 nor 22 get reduced down to a single digit.

A 8	B 14	C 65	D 7
E	F	G	H
I	J	K	L
M	N	O	P

Figure 4A

You may wonder why we create a sum of the numbers rather than add them up in a straight line. When we add in a straight line we run the risk of losing Master Numbers. My friend's birthday is an example of this. February 29, 1944, would be:

2+2+9+1+9+4+4 = 31, and 3+1 = 4.

Master Numbers give the person special capabilities, and it is important that these are represented in the yantra. This is why we always make a sum of the numbers, rather than add them up in a line.

We can now add up all the numbers in the top row and again bring them down to a single digit (unless we strike an 11 or 22 during the calculations). Let's go back to Crystal's yantra. Her top row reads: 8, 14, 65, and 7. These numbers total 94. Nine + 4 comes to 13, and 1+3 comes to 4. In Indian numerology this number is also interpreted, but it is usually ignored in the West.

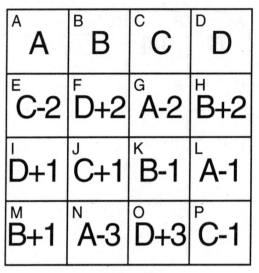

A A	B B	C C	D D
E C-2	F D+2	G A-2	H B+2
I D+1	J C+1	K B-1	L A-1
M B+1	N A-3	O D+3	P C-1

Figure 4B

The total of the top row is 94. That means that all of the other rows, horizontally, vertically, and diagonally, must also add up to 94.

We do this by using the chart shown in Figure 4B. It may look intimidating at first glance, but you'll find it very easy once you have constructed a few yantras. Let's complete Crystal's magic square.

In Figure 4A, Box A, we have the number 8. If you look at Box G in Figure 4B you will see that it says "A - 2." Box A is 8, so 8 - 2 is 6. Consequently, we put the number 6 in Box G of Crystal's chart. Box L is A - 1, so we put the number 7 in that box. Then we put the number 5 in Box N as A - 3 is 8 - 3 in Crystal's yantra. That completes all the numbers connected to Box A.

Now we work out the numbers associated with B. In the second row, H is B + 2. Crystal has the number 14 in

Box B, so B + 2 is 14 + 2 in her case. Fourteen + 2 is 16, so we put this number in Box H. Box K in the third row is B - 1. This is 14 - 1 in Crystal's case, so we put the number 13 in this box. We complete the B numbers by putting the number 15 in Box M (because it is B + 1.)

We now move on to Box C and insert the C numbers in the same way. Box E receives the number 63 (E is C - 2). Box J gets the number 66 (C + 1) and Box P gets 64 (C - 1). You are probably ahead of me by now. The D numbers complete Crystal's yantra. Box F gets number 9 (D + 2), Box I gets number 8 (D + 1), and Box O gets number 10 (D + 2).

You have now completed your first yantra (see Figure 4C). Check it out by adding up the horizontal, vertical, and diagonal lines. For instance, Boxes A, E, I, and M are 8, 63, 8, and 15. Adding them up gives us a total of 94. The Boxes E, F, G, and H are 63, 9, 6, and 16, which also total 94. The diagonal M, J, G, and D consists of 15, 66, 6, and 7 which again totals 94. Try the four corners, A, D, M, and P. This is 8, 7, 15, and 64, which also total 94. Let's try F, G, J and K: 9, 6, 66, and 13. They also add up to 94. So does A, B, E, and F. Let's try a 3 x 3 square: F, H, N, and P. This is 9, 16, 5, and 64. Amazingly, this also adds up to 94! Now you can start to see the fascination these magic squares have created for thousands of years.

Crystal can carry her yantra around with her as a talisman to attract good luck. She may choose to have it engraved on a pendant to wear around her neck or wrist. This is her personal yantra, constructed from her date of birth. The only other people in the whole world likely to carry the identical yantra would be those born on the exact same day, month, and year.

A 8	B 14	C 65	D 7
E 63	F 9	G 6	H 16
I 8	J 66	K 13	L 7
M 15	N 5	O 10	P 64

Figure 4C: Crystal's Yantra

As you can see, virtually no mathematics is required at all. If you can add or subtract the whole thing is very straightforward.

Let's try another one for practice. This time, we'll do my friend's yantra: February 29, 1944 (see Figure 4D).

The top row will consist of: 2, 29, 44, and 22. Box A is number 2. We look at Box G and find it is A - 2. Two - 2 = 0. Consequently, we write 0 (zero) in Box G. We put a 1 in Box L (A - 1). Now we come to Box N which is A - 3. Two - 3 equals minus 1, so we have to put -1 in Box N. You can get minus numbers, as you have just discovered. They have special meanings which will be explained in Chapter Six.

The B numbers are all straightforward. We put 31 in Box H (B + 2). Twenty-eight goes into Box K (B - 1), and 30 goes into Box M (B + 1).

A 2	B 29	C 44	D 22
E 42	F 24	G 0	H 31
I 23	J 45	K 28	L 1
M 30	N -1	O 25	P 43

Figure 4D

The C numbers go in the same way: 42 in Box E (C - 2), 45 in Box J (C + 1), and 43 in Box P (C - 1). The D numbers are: 24 in Box F, 23 in Box I, and 25 in Box O.

Check your mathematics by adding up a few of the horizontal, vertical, or diagonal rows. Boxes I, J, K, and L consist of 23, 45, 28, and 1 which total 97. Boxes N, J, F, and B consist of -1, 45, 24, and 29, which also total 97. Boxes M, J, G, and D contain 30, 45, 0, and 22, also a total of 97.

Practice drawing up yantras for your family and friends. The easiest way to memorize the formula is to construct as many charts as you can. In the next chapter we will start to interpret them.

chapter five

THE MEANINGS OF EACH BOX

Labeling each box with a letter of the alphabet makes the job of constructing the yantra much easier. However, this is not the reason for the letters. The real purpose is to code you to a keyword that tells you the area of the person's life the particular box refers to. Each letter acts as a mnemonic.

Boxes A, B, and C relate purely to the person's date of birth and are not interpreted later.

Box D has a key word of Destiny. In numerology the number in this box is known as the Life Path and reveals the person's purpose in life. As this is the most important number in numerology we pay close attention to the number in this box as it has relevance to all the other numbers.

Box E has two keywords: Enthusiasm and Energy. The number in this box shows the areas where the person will be most enthusiastic and energetic.

Box F relates to Family and Friends. The number here shows how the person relates to the important people in his or her life.

Box G stands for Generosity. The number in this box shows where the person will be most generous. This could relate to money, but may also relate to being generous with his or her time and energy.

Box H relates to Humanitarianism. The number here shows where the person is most likely to help others.

Box I has a keyword of Intuition. The number in this box shows where the person is most likely to use his or her intuition.

Box J has a keyword of *Joie de Vivre*, or Joy of Life. The number in this box shows where the person is happiest.

Box K relates to Karma. The number here reveals the karmic lessons the person has to pay back in this lifetime.

Box L has the keyword of Love. The number here shows the type of love relationship the subject is most likely to experience.

Box M relates to Money. The number here reveals how the person does financially.

Box N has a keyword of Nurture. The number in this box shows the areas the subject is likely to start and then gradually develop.

Box O relates to Opportunities. The number in this box shows the areas of life where the subject will have most opportunities.

Finally, Box P has a keyword of Philosophy. The number here shows the sort of faith or philosophy the person will develop as he or she goes through life.

To interpret the chart, all we have to do now is combine the numerological meaning of the numbers with the keyword of the letter in each box. We will cover some basic numerology in the next chapter.

chapter six

THE MEANINGS OF THE NUMBERS

Each number has a meaning, and this is combined with the keyword in each box to tell us the person's potential in thirteen different areas of life.

ONE

One is the number of individuation and independence. One wants to be in a position of leadership or authority. It is a strong, powerful number that seldom has need of the other numbers. One is highly independent and wants to do its own thing.

TWO

Two is the number of partnership, tact, and diplomacy. This number often acts as a peacemaker, smoothing troubled waters. It is able to make others feel at ease. It wants to get along with others and be liked. Unlike number one, it needs other people and works well in a partnership. One wants to get credit for its achievements. Number two is often satisfied with being in the number two position, "the power behind the throne."

THREE

Three wants to express the joys of life. It is essentially a number of communication, and it does this very ably in a light-hearted, carefree manner. It can be creative, but often lacks motivation and skims over the surface of different subjects, seldom learning anything in much depth. Three is positive and bounces back very quickly after any setback.

FOUR

Four is the number of hard work as well as system and order. This is the number of the plodder. Four always gets there in the end, but with slow and steady progress. It is able to establish system and order where none existed before. It works best within well-defined limits, and consequently is sometimes known as the number of restriction.

FIVE

Five stands for change and variety. This is often the rolling stone, enjoying many different experiences but always moving on and seldom standing still. This number often relates to travel as that is an extremely effective way of escaping day-to-day routine and of seeing new faces and places. Five feels unsettled when there is no avenue of escape and is likely to run whenever it seems that he or she is going to be restricted or hemmed in.

SIX

Six is the number of home and family responsibilities. This is one of the two caring, humanitarian numbers. Six loves helping others and is always the person others come to when things are out of balance in their lives. Six is always willing to give, and often finds it hard to fulfill his or her own needs because of the needs of others. Six is concerned mainly with family and finds its greatest happiness when surrounded by loved ones. Six is also a creative number.

SEVEN

This is the number of analysis and wisdom. Seven questions everything. It enjoys solitary pursuits and needs much time on its own to learn and understand the hidden truths. This number is "different" and seems to be on a different wavelength to the other numbers. This gives access to unique approaches, but can make it difficult for others to understand the seven's motivations. It also gives great originality. Ultimately, this number gives spirituality and wisdom.

EIGHT

This is the number of power and money. This number is highly motivated and wants to achieve its financial goals. It is strong, but can also be stubborn and rigid. It is prepared to work hard and long to achieve its goals. Fortunately, it is thick-skinned as it is prepared to ride roughshod over others if they attempt to get in the way. It is interesting to note that once eight has achieved its financial goals it can be very generous.

NINE

Nine is the second humanitarian number (the other is six). Six cares for people who are close. Nine is more universal, but at the same time more detached. It cares for people in general, rather than in particular. It loves helping, but does not want to become too involved with individual cases. Nine is also a creative number.

ELEVEN

Eleven is the first of the two Master Numbers. It gives enormous ability, and great ideas. Unfortunately, eleven does not often carry them out, nor are all the ideas practical. Eleven shows enormous promise, but seldom lives up to its potential. There is always a degree of nervous tension around number eleven, which can work against its best interests.

TWENTY-TWO

Twenty-two has the keyword of Master Builder. Twenty-two has the ideas of eleven, but possesses the practicality and capability to carry them out. It is capable of working on a national or international scale, and is happiest when working on something challenging and important. Like the eleven, nervous tension can be a problem. Success always takes considerable time for twenty-two. The potential is obvious to everyone except the twenty-two, who is likely to work at much less than its potential early on because it doesn't feel comfortable with high-level ideas and potentials. Once on track, nothing can stop the twenty-two.

Now you know the basic meanings of the numbers and the keywords of each box. We need to merge these together, before making a full interpretation.

chapter seven

BOX "D" – THE DESTINY NUMBER

The number in Box D is the Destiny number, the sum of the person's date of birth brought down to a single digit (unless, of course, it is an 11 or 22). You will remember that the date of birth is brought down to a single digit by creating a sum, rather than by adding the numbers up sideways.

The resulting number is known as the person's Life Path and it represents the person's purpose in life. Very few people are aware of their purpose, so knowledge of this number can be extremely useful.

ONE

Someone with a Life Path number of one is going to have to learn to stand on his or her own two feet and achieve independence. This is not an easy lesson to learn. Many people on this path start out in life by being dependent, rather than independent, and gradually gain confidence as they mature. The ultimate position for someone on this path is in a leadership role. This could be in management, self-employment, or some other position where the person has sufficient responsibility.

TWO

A person with a Life Path of two is going to have to learn the lesson of diplomacy. This is an enjoyable path, as the person will instinctively be able to make others feel at ease. However, he or she will be overly sensitive at times, and will have to learn to handle his or her emotions. This number is naturally intuitive, and the sensitivity is often channeled into psychic areas.

THREE

Someone on this path will be learning creative self-expression. This can come out in a variety of ways: talking, writing, music, etc. With most people it comes out as verbal communication. This path is a pleasant one as there is a certain lightness attached to number three. The risk is that the person will dabble and fail to develop his or her talents.

FOUR

This is the number of system and order. Someone on a four Life Path has to learn to establish and maintain system and order. He or she will have to pay attention to details, and work hard and long when required. It is not an easy path. The person will see others taking short cuts and enjoying frivolous activities, and could resent the necessity of working so hard. However, the hard work does ultimately pay off.

FIVE

Someone on this path has to learn to harness continual change and variety. Young people on this path are likely to worry loved ones with their erratic behavior and inability to settle down. However, once they find the right track, their progress can be remarkable. People on a five Life Path always need something exciting to look forward to. Generally, they try to find an exciting, varied career. Otherwise, they find the variety they crave with a series of unusual hobbies or interests.

SIX

Someone on this Life Path will be learning the lesson of responsibility, particularly family responsibility. They will enjoy being with and caring for people they love. They need to make sure that their own needs are met though, and that they do not become a doormat for everyone else. This Life Path can be a highly rewarding one, and the person is likely to give—and receive back—a great deal of love. Six is also a highly creative, artistic number and people on this path receive enormous pleasure from pursuing creative activities.

SEVEN

Seven is a very powerful Life Path. People on this path have to learn to analyze and discriminate. It is an introspective path and they will need to spend much time on their own, without feeling lonely. As they progress through life they will gradually build up a philosophy and a faith, ultimately gaining wisdom and knowledge.

EIGHT

People on this Life Path need to learn to handle money and large undertakings. They need to find something challenging that has the potential for financial reward. They will be rigid and fixed in their views, and need to learn to be more flexible. They must be scrupulously honest, as a greedy eight will inevitably learn the hard way through a loss of some sort.

NINE

People on this Life Path need to learn to become humanitarians. It is a positive path, but many on this track resent the need to be forever giving. The greatest rewards come from giving with no thought of any return. This is a hard lesson to learn, and young people on this path often try to turn it around, becoming takers and users rather than givers. Doing this provides no satisfaction. Nine, along with three and six, is a creative number, providing considerable potential. Many nines do their giving through some form of creativity.

THE TWO MASTER NUMBERS

In numerology, people with Master Numbers are regarded as being "old souls." In other words, they have lived through many previous lifetimes and have gradually evolved and developed. They are likely to have already mastered the easier lessons, and now, in this lifetime, have to face some of the more challenging ones. They are likely to spend a large part of their lives trying to harness the special energies attached to a Master Number, and consequently generally reach their peak late in life. Of course, many find it too hard to handle and work at a lower level. An eleven might bring it down to a two, and a twenty-two to a four. They would be aware that they were achieving only a minute fraction of what they were capable of doing, but would rather remain in mediocrity than try to harness the energies of their Master Number.

ELEVEN

Eleven is the number of inspiration and enlightenment. People on this path have great dreams. Their Master number gives them access to many ideas and concepts. They need to carefully evaluate these ideas, and accept only the ones that are practical. They spend much time in daydreams, and need to ensure that they also spend sufficient time in making their dreams a reality.

TWENTY-TWO

People on this Life Path are able to accomplish anything once they learn how to harness the nervous energy that is always present around Master Numbers. They have access to the same ideas as elevens, but have the practicality to make good use of them. This number is known as the Master Builder, and people on this path literally can achieve anything they set their minds on, ideally something on a large scale.

chapter eight

THE OTHER BOXES

Box D stands on its own, and is extremely important as it reveals the person's Life Path. The other boxes all relate to different aspects of the person's personality. The numbers inside each box tell us how the person expresses him or herself in the particular area of life represented by the box.

First, we have to reduce the number in each box to a single digit, except, of course, in the case of Master Numbers. Here is an example.

Assume we are constructing a yantra for a man born on March 20, 1974 (see Figure 8A). D is already a single digit, as we reduced it when doing the necessary mathematics to work out his Life Path. Box E, though, is number 72. In this case, for interpretation purposes only, we add the two digits together, which gives us 9 (7+2 = 9). We do not alter

A 3	B 20	C 74	D 8
E 72	F 10	G 1	H 22
I 9	J 75	K 19	L 2
M 21	N 0	O 11	P 73

Figure 8A

the number 72 in the yantra. Boxes F and G are already single digits, so we leave them as they are. H is 22. Do we add the two 2s together, or leave it as it is? Right, we leave it as it is, as 22 is a Master Number. Box I is a single digit again, but Box J is 75. For interpretation, this is reduced to a 3 (7+5 = 12, and 1+2 = 3). In the same way Box K is reduced to a 1, Box M to a 3, and Box P to a 1.

By doing this, we can interpret any number at all, once we know the meanings of numbers 1 to 9, plus 11 and 22. Usually you will be reducing a two-digit number to a single digit. However, as we get nearer to the year 2000, you will come across three-digit numbers from time to time. These are simply reduced to a two-digit number, and then down to a single digit.

Now we can start interpreting each box.

NUMBERS IN BOX E

Keywords: Enthusiasm and Energy

One

People with number one in Box E put a great deal of enthusiasm and energy into doing their own thing. They set their own individual goals and go after them with a great deal of determination. They are happiest left to their own devices, with little input from others.

Two

People with number two in Box E put their enthusiasm and energy into close relationships. They enjoy being with people and want to be close to the people they like. They have a need to be liked by others. They make an effort with all of their relationships and invariably see the positive side of people they meet. They can also put enthusiasm and energy into psychic development.

Three

With number three in Box E you have a real enthusiast! People who enjoy having a good time. They put energy and considerable enthusiasm into entertaining and being entertained. They are inclined to dissipate their energies by attempting too many activities at the same time. They can be creative, but often lack motivation to finish what they start.

Four

Four is the number of hard work, and people with this number in Box E enjoy a challenge. They put a great deal of enthusiasm and energy into achieving worthwhile goals. They get little pleasure out of things that happen easily:

they need a challenge, the harder the better. As worthwhile goals usually take a great deal of time, the enthusiasm carries them through the slower, duller parts, and is still there when they emerge triumphantly at the far end.

Five

These people put a great deal of enthusiasm and energy into doing things that are exciting and different. They crave the unusual, the offbeat. They get enormous pleasure out of planning a trip, and then doing it. They are inclined to take risks at times in their efforts to escape the humdrum and mundane. These people remain young at heart throughout their lives.

Six

People with number six in Box E put their enthusiasm and energy into home and family life. They enjoy puttering around the house and love family activities. They are prepared to do anything for loved ones and are inclined to be self-sacrificing at times. They enjoy beautifying their surroundings and put a great deal of energy into anything they regard as being creative.

Seven

People with the number seven in Box E put their energies and enthusiasm into learning and spiritual growth. They love being on their own to ponder deep mysteries and to grow in knowledge and wisdom. They pour their energies into activities and interests that other people might see as being slightly unusual.

Eight

As eight is the money number, these people put a great deal of enthusiasm and energy into making money and being involved in large-scale undertakings. They enjoy making plans and then going out and achieving them. They are motivated by money and work well in careers where their efforts are rewarded in straight-out financial terms. Commission sales is a good field.

These people can also put a great deal of enthusiasm into spending money, usually on themselves.

Nine

People with number nine in Box E put a great deal of time, effort, and enthusiasm into helping others less fortunate. Nine is a very giving number, and these people are happiest when giving of themselves for a worthwhile cause. These humanitarian motives can be directed toward plants, animals, or humans. We need as many of these people as possible in the world today.

Eleven

People with number eleven in Box E pour their enthusiasm and energy into idealistic pursuits. They are happiest when doing—or thinking about—worthy aims that could benefit humanity as a whole. As they are so idealistic, their ideas are often unpractical, and they need to share their ideas with others to gauge how effective they will be. These people spend a great deal of time in pleasant daydreams.

Twenty-Two

As twenty-two is the Master Builder, these people put their enthusiasm and energy into large-scale enterprises that can benefit humanity. Their enthusiasm and energy make them totally tireless once they have decided on a worthwhile goal.

NUMBERS IN BOX F

Keywords: Family and Friends

One

People with number one in this box love their family and friends. However, they see themselves as individuals with definite needs to be met, and they will satisfy these needs ahead of any family wants. In a sense, a one does not need anyone else, as one is self-sufficient. Consequently, they often appear to be selfish, egotistical, and demanding to others. However, they do not see these qualities in themselves.

Two

People with a two in this position love being surrounded by friends and family. They enjoy the special warmth, love, and security created by close friends and family. They go out of their way to befriend others, and to make sure that everyone in the family is getting along well with everyone else. For them to be happy, they need everyone else to be happy, too.

Three

People with the number three in this position are the organizers of the family. They enjoy arranging parties and other entertainments. They shy away from deep, involved discussions, preferring more light-hearted conversation that does not probe into things too deeply. They are warm-hearted, friendly, and fun to be around. Don't expect them to take on much responsibility, though.

Four

People with the number four in Box F are the workers in the family. They make sure that everyone stays in contact, they keep the family tree up to date, and they don't hesitate to let everyone know the hard work they are doing. They enjoy constant praise for all their efforts. They can be exhausting to be around, but fulfill a very valuable role in the family. They are often respected, rather than loved.

Five

People with a five in Box F enjoy surprising their family and friends with what they do. They might arrange a surprise party, or call their friends at strange hours suggesting they accompany them on a trip to Mt. Everest. They are full of ideas of what the family could do. The fact that their ideas are often extravagant seldom enters their thoughts. Things are lively when these people are around.

Six

Six is the number of home and family, so it harmonizes well with the values of Box F. People with this number here are family-minded, caring, and supportive. They love their friends and family with total devotion. They are willing to do whatever is necessary for the wellbeing of loved ones. Their only fault is that they can be overly protective and stifle any attempts at independence by members of the family.

Seven

People with seven in Box F make wonderful housekeepers. They can be perfectionists, though, which would annoy other members of the family. They are loving, but slightly detached, and find it hard to express their innermost feelings. Although they love family and friends they also need quite a bit of time on their own.

Eight

People with eight in Box F enjoy making money with friends and family. A family-owned business, with the number eight in the president's chair, is ideal. At times money-making comes ahead of the family needs, and this can cause dissension. These people can become workaholics and may need to be forced to spend time in leisure activities with loved ones.

These people are also likely to inherit money.

Nine

People with the number nine in Box F love their family and friends, but often spend more time helping strangers than the people they care for most. They are likely to become involved in different humanitarian causes, while ignoring the needs of family. Once they become aware of this, they instantly drop everything to help the loved ones, and then return to their favorite charity. They make friends easily, but often these are with people who want to lean on them.

Eleven

These people are idealistic and have a glorious vision of what family life and friendship should be like. As reality can never hope to match this dream, they are constantly disappointed. They have an incredible intuition and know when something is wrong with someone they care about, and they enjoy helping them.

Twenty-Two

It is impossible to have the number twenty-two in this position, which is fortunate. It would be impossible to live with someone who was just about perfect in every way.

NUMBERS IN BOX G

Keyword: Generosity

One

People with the number one in Box G are generous in their own way. They can be very generous with causes they support, but slow to support activities that do not appeal as much to them.

Two

People with number two in this position are generous for two reasons: first, they like to help others, and, just as important, they want to be liked. By being generous they have more chance of being liked by others. Consequently, they are likely to be more generous when others are around to see the generosity. They are particularly generous with their time and energy when it comes to helping loved ones.

Three

Threes are generous in a casual sort of way. If they have money in their pocket, they will donate it to any worthwhile cause. They can also be very generous with their time if the activity is enjoyable.

Four

People with number four in Box G are careful with their money and will want to be sure that the cause is worthwhile before contributing. They do not expect a free lunch themselves, and are loathe to give money away too freely. However, if the cause is worthwhile they can be very generous.

Five

Fives are generous in a haphazard way. They may give a lot of money to one cause and very little to another that was equally as deserving. Their contributions can be spread over a wide range of causes. They are not so generous with their time. They hate being confined or restricted, and even being tied down for an afternoon is hard for them. If you want fives to assist you, make them think that it is their idea, and then they will be very willing to help.

Six

People with a six in Box G are particularly generous with family and loved ones. They are caring people and will give generously to any worthy cause. However, they make sure the needs of their loved ones are met first. They are inclined to be a soft touch to a sad story.

Seven

Sevens can be generous if the cause appeals to their beliefs or philosophy. They are careful about giving to causes they are not familiar with, as they have heard numerous stories about money being intended for charity being used up in administration, rather than in helping others. They can be very generous in lending a helping hand when needed.

Eight

Number eight in this position makes an interesting combination. Eights want to make money, rather than give it away. Yet, eights can be very generous if the cause is deserving. They are likely to investigate the cause first, as they do not give money away lightly. If the cause is worthwhile, they can be extremely generous benefactors. Whenever possible they like to receive recognition for their generosity.

Nine

As nine is a giving number, it is extremely generous when found in this position. Nines love nothing more than helping others, so can be generous in giving of their time and energy as well as money.

Eleven

It is impossible for this number to be in Box G.

Twenty-Two

This number can not appear in this position.

NUMBERS IN BOX H

Keyword: Humanitarianism

One

People with a one in Box H are humanitarians, but in their own way. They would rather help individually than be part of an organized charity or philanthropic organization. When working with others they need to be in the spotlight or in a leadership role.

Two

Two in Box H is a good combination. Twos get a great deal of pleasure from helping others, and make natural humanitarians. This helping is likely to be mainly with family and close friends.

Three

Number three in Box H is an interesting combination. Threes love communicating, and can help others with their company and bright conversation. They find it harder, though, to actually dig in and help others in a more tangible way.

Four

When fours are helping others they are prepared to work hard and do everything necessary to assist the people they are working for. They enjoy working for humanitarian causes that they believe in, and do not necessarily want to receive recognition for their contribution.

Five

Fives get along well with people and make natural, if haphazard, humanitarians. They get impatient, though, if their efforts do not bring instant results. Sometimes they get themselves involved in too many different humanitarian activities, and end up running around in circles helping no one.

Six

Six is one of the two humanitarian numbers (the other is nine). Sixes love helping others, particularly people they care for, and they welcome opportunities to become involved in humanitarian activities. They also enjoy helping animals and plants and frequently become involved in organizations that help endangered species or sick animals.

Seven

Sevens enjoy the idea of helping others, but are somewhat detached and find it hard to help directly. They find it easier to be involved in the back-room activities, rather than actually go out and assist. In their own way they help many people, but you would have to know them very well to be aware of it.

Eight

Eights are more likely to help with a donation rather than jump in and help in other ways. Once involved though, they will work long and hard to help any cause they believe in.

Nine

Nines are natural humanitarians. They thoroughly enjoy working for others and are happy to assist in any way they can. These humanitarian desires frequently show themselves in their choice of occupation, and any field involving helping others would be suitable. Careers such as teaching, nursing, and counseling are obvious choices, but they will use their humanitarian skills in any field they enter.

Eleven

Elevens love the idea of helping others. They have great ideas about all the things that could and should be done to make this world a better place for everyone. Unfortunately, they do not always act on these fine motives. Once involved though, with continual encouragement from others, they make wonderful humanitarians.

Twenty-Two

Twenty-twos enjoy helping others. Their position is likely to be as an organizer, rather than as a worker. Their leadership skills are a great advantage when it comes to helping others, and they have the ability to inspire and motivate the volunteers under them.

NUMBERS IN BOX I

Keyword: Intuition

One

One is a logical number, so people with this number in Box I are inclined to rely more on logic than their intuition. All the same, they do get flashes of inspiration when it comes to something they see as being important. They are more likely to call it a "hunch" or a "gut feeling," rather than intuition.

Two

People with two in this position rely very much on their natural, strong intuition. They take it for granted as being an essential part of their life. They are especially intuitive when it comes to people they care about, and often know instantly when something is wrong with a friend or family member.

Three

Three is a strong, logical number. In a moment of crisis, people with the number three in this position are more likely to act on cold, hard logic rather than trust their inner voice. However, when doing something creative, they can often move from logic into an intuitive state which enhances their work. In other words, they move from left-brain thinking to right-brain.

Four

People with four in Box I will listen to their intuition, but will also evaluate the situation logically before acting. They pride themselves on being logical thinkers, but actually rely on their intuition more than they care to admit.

Five

People with the number five in this position are casual about their intuition. They get intuitive flashes about all sorts of things. They also use logic over a wide area. Both logic and intuition are used in a haphazard way. Fives live in the future more than the present and their intuition often helps them make the right choice. This is one reason why number five is often regarded as being a lucky number.

Six

People with a six in Box I get strong intuitive feelings about their home and family. They intuitively know the right time to call or visit someone in the family who needs help. Their intuition ranges over a wide area, but is used most frequently with loved ones.

Seven

People with a seven in Box I combine spirituality and intuition as they gradually grow in knowledge and wisdom. Their logical minds can sometimes lose the intuition, but when they slow down enough to listen, their abilities in this field can be highly impressive.

Eight

Eight is a logical number, but people with eight in this position are able to use their intuition in assessing the worth of any money-making venture. They examine all the facts and figures, but often it will be their intuition that provides the right answer. Early on in life, logic is likely to win, but gradually they learn to accept and trust their "quiet, inner voice."

Nine

Nine is the humanitarian number and people with this number in Box I are able to use their intuition in helping others. They can sometimes remain quite detached, but at the same time know when it is time to visit someone who needs their help or advice. They have a knack of being in the right position at the right time to help others. This is because of their fine intuition.

Eleven

It is impossible to have an eleven in this position.

Twenty-Two

It is impossible to have twenty-two in this position.

NUMBERS IN BOX J

Keywords: Joie de Vivre

One

People with the number one in this position are happiest when they are doing their own thing, usually entirely on their own. This could be in any area of life. A hobby is likely to be something like stamp collecting, for instance. A sport might be archery. Although there may be other people around, the person is doing his or her own thing as an individual.

Two

People with the number two in Box J are happiest when surrounded by the people they care for. They enjoy family outings and other special times with loved ones.

Three

People with the number three in this position enjoy being with people and having a good time. They enjoy social activities and anything that entertains them. They enjoy conversation and creative hobbies.

Four

People with number four in this position enjoy having a challenge, something to work toward and achieve. They have a tendency to be workaholics and often need to be forced into taking time off for rest and relaxation.

Five

Five is the number of freedom and variety and people with the number five here are happiest when they have something exciting to look forward to. They enjoy travel, meeting new people, and enjoying new and different experiences.

Six

People with six in this position are happiest when involved in family activities. They enjoy helping people and love being needed by others. They also enjoy creative activities.

Seven

People with the number seven in this position are happiest when left to their own devices. They enjoy learning and thinking about the mysteries of the universe. They have mystical tendencies and often lose track of time when engaged in contemplation or meditation.

Eight

People with an eight in this position are happiest when making money, or when thinking of money-making ideas. They also enjoy spending money, as long as they see the purchase as being worthwhile and not frivolous.

Nine

People with the number nine in Box J are happiest when helping people less fortunate than themselves. They enjoy working for charities and philanthropic organizations and are always willing to lend a helping hand. They also love creative activities and enjoy giving away what they produce.

Eleven

People with the number eleven in Box J are happiest when thinking about large-scale plans and dreams. These ideas usually remain as dreams, but elevens get enormous pleasure out of them even though they know deep down that they are unlikely to achieve them. Once sufficiently motivated, they also enjoy acting out their dreams and making them happen. The biggest problem they face is deciding which dream out of many to pursue.

Twenty-Two

People with the number twenty-two in this position are happiest when pursuing a worthwhile goal. They want to do things on a large scale so the goal has to be worthy of their abilities. They get much more pleasure out of the progress than from the accomplishment itself.

NUMBERS IN BOX K

Keyword: Karma

One

People with a one in Box K failed to stand on their own two feet in a previous incarnation. This means they are likely to start off this incarnation by being dependent, and gradually have to learn independence.

Two

People with a two in this position failed to use their intuition in a past life. Consequently, they will find it hard to trust their intuition in the early part of this lifetime, and will only gradually come to recognize and make use of it.

These people also made mistakes with close relationships, and will have to work hard at this area of life to avoid disappointment in this lifetime.

Three

People with the number three in this position were superficial and frivolous in a previous lifetime. In this life they need to learn when to be serious and when to be light-hearted.

Four

People with the number four in this position were lazy in a past lifetime. Consequently, in this life they may sometimes feel as if they are working twice as hard as other people to get to the same place. As they progress through life and pay off this karmic debt, every area of their life gradually becomes easier.

Five

People with the number five in this position wasted time in a past lifetime. They probably overindulged in a wide range of sensual activities. The lesson is for them to learn to use their time wisely. This is not an easy lesson, and it usually takes many years before they realize that time is slipping away.

Six

People with the number six in this position ignored their family responsibilities in a previous incarnation. They need to learn to love and care for their family in this lifetime.

Seven

People with number seven in this position failed to develop spiritually in a previous lifetime. Consequently it is important for them to build up a faith or philosophy in this lifetime. They are likely to have a questioning, slightly skeptical approach to spiritual matters early on in life.

Eight

People with the number eight in this position misused money in a previous lifetime. They may have had plenty and squandered it, or perhaps even misappropriated money. As a result, they will have to work extremely hard to progress financially in this lifetime until the karmic debt is repaid.

Nine

People with the number nine in Box K avoided helping others in a past incarnation. As a result, they will find it hard to progress in this lifetime until they learn to help and care for others. Once the lesson is learned they are likely to become true humanitarians.

Eleven

People with an eleven in this position were given good opportunities in a past life, but failed to seize them, probably through a lack of confidence or a fear of failure. They need to ensure that they do not hold themselves back when the right opportunities come along in this lifetime.

Twenty-Two

People with the number twenty-two in this position misused responsibility in a previous lifetime. They need to accept responsibility in this incarnation and work hard and long to achieve something really worthwhile.

NUMBERS IN BOX L

Keyword: Love

One

The number one in this position is an indication of one major relationship that grows and develops. People with number one in Box L can sometimes be self-centered, but generally manage to find partners who can live with this.

Two

People with the number two in this position make close, supportive partners. They can communicate with their partners using their highly-developed intuition. This also lets them know instantly when something is not going well or is worrying their partner.

Three

People with the number three in this position need partners who enjoy conversation and plenty of entertainment. Although they may flirt at times, this is usually for show and is not serious.

Four

People with the number four in this position work hard at their relationships. They may not be the most exciting of partners, but are always good providers and care deeply for their loved ones. They are faithful and affectionate.

Five

People with the number five in Box L need space and room. They hate being confined, even in a close relationship. They are likely to run at the first sign of being hemmed in. However, they make excellent partners and exciting lovers, providing they are allowed room for outside interests as well.

Six

People with the number six in this position are happiest inside a good, strong, loving relationship. They do not feel complete unless they are surrounded by their loved ones. This is usually their partner and children, but can also include very close friends. They are caring, and enjoy expressing their love and affection.

Seven

People with the number seven in this position need time on their own, and require partners who will respect this. Given the right relationship they can be very loving in thought and action, but always find it hard to express these feelings in words.

Eight

People with the number eight in Box L often do well financially from the right loving relationship. They might marry into money, or perhaps form a business as well as a love relationship with someone. These partnerships are not likely to be as romantic as some, but are usually long-lasting and happy.

Nine

People with a nine in this position make considerate and highly romantic partners. They enjoy pleasing and surprising their mates with tokens of their love. They need to be careful in choosing partners though, as they are inclined to fall in love with the idea of being in love and make the wrong choices. Given the right partner though, these are very strong relationships.

Eleven

People with the number eleven in this position are idealistic and easily disappointed. They need to choose their partners carefully as they fall in and out of love very easily. They are caring and loving. They express their emotions freely and need partners who are strong and supportive.

Twenty-Two

It is impossible to have twenty-two in this position.

NUMBERS IN BOX M

Keyword: Money

One

People with a number one in this position like complete mastery of their money. They are prepared to work hard to make it but want to be sure that they are rewarded adequately. Many people with a one in this position work for themselves, as this ensures that they are in total control of their money.

Two

People with the number two in this position are able to use their intuition when it comes to making and/or spending money. This means that they can instinctively tell if a proposal is good or bad, even when all the figures look good. However, they may have to learn the hard way to trust their quiet inner voice.

Three

People with a three in Box M are able to make money from their communication skills, usually their talking abilities.

For instance, they would make good sales people, entertainers or teachers. They are good at coming up with money-making ideas, but often lack the motivation to carry them through.

Four

People with the number four in this position like being in solid, respectable occupations and gradually work their way up to responsible positions. They expect to work hard for what they get, and take great pleasure in each step of the journey.

Five

People with a five in this position make good wheeler-dealers. They like change and variety and usually become involved in several different careers as they progress through their lives. They are happiest when self-employed as they do not like being told what to do. Their love of variety means their careers often involve travel.

Six

People with a six in Box M enjoy stable occupations with good job security. Work always comes second to home and family concerns. They are likely to benefit financially from other members of the family. This is usually an inheritance.

Seven

People with a seven in this position enjoy scientific or technical occupations. They enjoy the research and study that is involved. They seldom earn as much as they could, as they seek job satisfaction ahead of financial rewards.

Eight

Eight is the money number, so is well sited in this box. People with an eight in this position work well in financial fields or in self-employment. If not self-employed they will have a responsible position in someone else's business. They work hard and are good at making money. They need to ensure that they have other interests outside of money as it can easily become an obsession.

Nine

People with a nine in this position can make money working for humanitarian organizations. Their desire to help others can sometimes make them self-sacrificing, so they can be overly generous when it comes to money. They see money as a means of exchange, rather than an end in itself.

Eleven

People with the number eleven in this position can make money from their ideas. They often work best in a partnership with people who have more push and drive than they do. They work well in humanitarian areas, such as education and social welfare. They also do well in creative fields. They do not usually do well in business.

Twenty-Two

People with this number in Box M have the potential to make as much money as they wish. They need worthwhile goals that they believe in. They seldom work for selfish ends, preferring to do things they see as being worthwhile for humanity as a whole.

NUMBERS IN BOX N

Keyword: Nurture

One

People with number one in this position enjoy starting things and watching them grow. They are more likely to start a business, for instance, rather than buy an existing one. They are often better at starting than finishing, but their interests are important while they last.

Two

People with a two in Box N use their powerful intuitions to help and support others. They are caring, sympathetic people who derive great pleasure from watching other people succeed.

Three

People with the number three in this position are able to build people up with their gift of easy conversation. They are able to inspire others with their words. They are creative and, when pushed, can develop their own talents a long way.

Four

People with the number four in this position are able to work hard and long to support and build up anything that they believe in. Patience is their strong suit, so they are happy to wait years, if necessary, to see success come to something they have supported and worked for.

Five

People with the number five in this position help and advise people in all sorts of different areas. Their advice is sound and well meant, but they have often gone before the results are apparent. They need to be encouraged to nurture something for themselves, and to follow it through to completion.

Six

People with the number six in this position are happiest when supporting and nurturing people they care for. They make wonderful parents, although they sometimes find it hard to allow their children much independence. They are able to work hard at creative interests and enjoy watching their own progress.

Seven

People with the number seven in Box N enjoy mental challenges, finding out what makes different things work and understanding the hidden truths. When something interests them they are able to start small and gradually build it up into a major project.

Eight

People with the number eight in this position are able to take very small undertakings and gradually build them up into lucrative endeavors. They enjoy taking on projects that they feel will make money, and are prepared to nurture them for as long as necessary, providing the potential to make money remains.

Nine

People who have number nine in this position enjoy helping and supporting groups of people. This could be a club, where they would work hard and long as organizer, or a philanthropic organization, or any other field where they feel their contribution will help others. They are wonderful at raising other people's self-esteem.

Eleven

It is impossible to have number eleven in this position.

Twenty-Two

It is impossible to have the number twenty-two in this position.

NUMBERS IN BOX O

Keyword: Opportunities

One

People with a number one in Box O will make their own opportunities. They prefer little input from others, and enjoy doing their own thing.

Two

It is impossible to have a two in this box.

Three

People with the number three in Box O will find their greatest opportunities in some form of self-expression. They are likely to have a creative talent, especially one involving communication with others. They will also find opportunities through talking with others.

Four

People with the number four in Box O will find their best opportunities close at hand. They need to work within the limits they find, and will also find their opportunities there. They are likely to make mistakes when seeking opportunities outside their field of expertise.

Five

People with the number five in this position find opportunities everywhere. They find many more of these than they can ever use. A problem is that they are likely to try too many different opportunities, rather than concentrating on one or two.

Six

People with the number six in this position find their best opportunities with, or through, family and friends. They are generous when it comes to sharing their opportunities with others. They are also given a number of creative opportunities.

Seven

People with the number seven in Box O will be given opportunities to develop spiritually and grow in knowledge and wisdom. They are likely to ignore the spiritual opportunities early in life, usually preferring the opportunities that appear in scientific or technical areas. However, the spiritual side gets stronger and stronger and cannot be ignored indefinitely.

Eight

People with the number eight in this position are given opportunities to both make and spend money. They have many opportunities to invest in money-making schemes, and are shrewd when it comes to assessing the worth of these plans. They are also given many opportunities to spend their money, and this is normally done in areas that give both pleasure and status.

Nine

People with the number nine in this position will be given many opportunities to help people less fortunate than themselves. They enjoy giving help and support to others and usually look for opportunities to serve.

Eleven

People with the number eleven in this position will come up with many opportunities in every area of their lives. They need to evaluate these opportunities carefully and utilize only the ones that are likely to benefit them. Once motivated, they are able to make their daydreams practical.

Twenty-Two

It is impossible to have twenty-two in this position.

NUMBERS IN BOX P

Keyword: Philosophy

One

People with a number one in this position gradually build up their own personal philosophy as they go through life. It is likely to be a questioning sort of faith, that they gradually formulate as a result of the experiences they meet.

Two

People with the number two in this position build up a faith and philosophy based on their intuitive insights. They are caring people who use their inner voice in every area of their lives.

Three

People with the number three in Box P have a philosophy of life that they work out logically, questioning everything. They often fail to explore subjects in great depth, preferring a superficial glance, and their philosophy is likely to be an amalgam of everything they have explored.

Four

People with number four in this position spend time and effort building up their personal philosophies. They study and evaluate carefully, gradually building up a philosophy that continues to develop all the way through their lives.

Five

People with five in this position change their personal philosophies from time to time as they encounter new experiences. They love exploring new areas and gradually build up a faith and philosophy after evaluating everything they have learned.

Six

People with a six in Box P build up a faith and philosophy built around the sanctity of the family unit. They are likely to believe that they will be together for eternity.

Seven

People with a seven in Box P are spiritual, philosophically-inclined people. Their faith, whatever it may be, is strong and constant, and grows all the way through life.

Eight

People with the number eight in this position have a philosophy based around the hard work ethic. They believe in getting rewarded for their contributions. As they live so much in the material world, they do not usually give much thought to the spiritual side of life until they reach their retirement years.

Nine

People with the number nine in this position build up a philosophy based on helping others. Behind a slightly detached exterior they are true humanitarians who are willing to help everyone.

Eleven

People with the number eleven in this position are idealistic, which makes them prone to many disappointments. They gradually build up a philosophy of life based on their intuition and powerful insight.

Twenty-Two

People with number twenty-two in this position want to make a mark on the world. They would like to leave the world a better place than they found it. They are idealistic but practical. They gradually build up a strong, powerful faith and philosophy which enables them to handle anything that life may throw at them.

NEGATIVE NUMBERS

Keyword: Stress Number

Every so often you will construct a yantra for someone and find they have negative (minus) numbers in one or more boxes. These numbers are known as Negative, or Stress, Numbers. They indicate an area of life that the person needs to concentrate upon, as this is where he or she is most likely to make mistakes.

Instead of working on the positive side of the number, these people are inclined to act on the negative. The number one, for example, has keywords of independence and attainment. A negative one means virtually the opposite. It is an indication of dependence and lack of self-esteem.

People with Negative Numbers should be encouraged to work towards attaining the positive attributes of the number.

This may all seem like a great deal to learn. In fact, it is not. Once you know the meanings of the numbers as described in Chapter Six, all you need do is combine them with the keywords for each box, and you will automatically know all the possible combinations.

chapter nine

READING THE YANTRA

We now know how to construct a yantra and understand what each box means. Now we'll interpret one. Let's assume we are doing a reading for a woman who was born on March 12, 1975 (see Figure 9A). Let's call her Danielle.

We start by looking at her Life Path number which is a 1 (Box D).

"Your Destiny number is a 1," we might say. "This means that you have the ability to stand on your own two feet and really achieve something. Your ultimate position is at the top of any field you go into. You need to aim high. Set some goals for yourself and then go after them.

"You also have a 1 in the box that relates to enthusiasm and energy (Box E). This means that you put a great deal of yourself into achieving your goals. Make sure that you

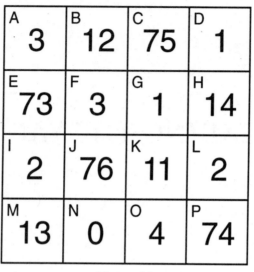

Figure 9A

know what you want, and then start moving. You have more than enough energy and enthusiasm to take you there.

"Your family and friends are indicated by this number 3 (F). This means that you express yourself best with the people you care for most. You enjoy good, fun times with your friends.

"The next box (G) shows your generosity. With the number 1 there, you are generous but in your own way. You can be generous with your time and energy as well as money.

"This box represents your humanitarian qualities (H). You have the number 5 in this position. This means that you are very much a humanitarian, but you do it in a sometimes rather haphazard manner. You may help someone over here, then a group over there, and someone back there, and so on. You are more likely to support a range of humanitarian causes, rather than just one.

"The next box (I) represents your intuition. You have the perfect number there. Two is the psychic, intuitive number. This shows that you have plenty of potential in this area, and could develop your intuition a long, long way.

"The next box (J) is an interesting one as it shows what you really enjoy doing. A 4 in this box shows that you get great pleasure from hard work and challenges. Most people hate the idea of hard work, but you actually seek opportunities, as long as you can see the hard work paying off.

"You have a Master Number in this box (K). This is the box of karma. If you believe in reincarnation, it is things that were not done in a previous lifetime. A Master Number in this position shows that last time around you had some wonderful opportunities but failed to take advantage of them. You were probably a daydreamer who was lost in a world of pleasant fantasies. It shows that in this life you need to harness your dreams and do something with them.

"The next box (L) is the area of love, and here you have the perfect number—a 2. Two is the number of close relationships. It does not mean two major relationships. It is an indication of one major love that lasts all the way through this incarnation.

"The box down in the corner (M) is the position for money. Here you have the number 4 again. Four is the number of hard work, so most of your money will come through plain hard work and good money management.

"In the next box (N) you have a zero. This is the box of helping activities grow and blossom. A zero rating here is neither good nor bad. The absence of a specific number means there is no aspect of your life which encompasses this particular area.

"After that, we have the box of opportunities (O). Here is yet another 4. This shows that you will have to make your own opportunities and will then have to work hard to achieve them. Fortunately, you enjoy doing this. (This is because the number 4 is also in box J.)

"Finally, we reach the last box, Danielle (P). Here we have another Master Number. This box reflects your philosophy of life. The 11 shows that you are inspirational, idealistic, and caring. You have the potential to inspire others with what you do."

Here is another example. This time it is for a man called John who was born on January 17, 1950 (see Figure 9B).

"You have a Life Path of 6, John (Box D). This shows that you are a caring, humanitarian kind of person, someone who enjoys helping others. You are likely to be happiest inside a good, strong, solid relationship. Your home and family life is likely to be one of the most important factors in your life.

"Box E represents your enthusiasms and energy. Here you have the number 3 (4+8 = 12, and 1+2 = 3). This shows that you put a great deal of enthusiasm and energy into expressing yourself. This could be singing, dancing, talking, writing—anything, in fact, that you personally consider to be creative. It will most likely be talking.

"Eight is the money number and you have it here in Box F. This means one of two things. You can benefit financially from family and friends. Or, you can spend money

A 1	B 17	C 50	D 6
E 48	F 8	G -1	H 19
I 7	J 51	K 16	L 0
M 18	N -2	O 9	P 49

Figure 9B

on family and friends. Usually, though, it means you benefit, so you'll no doubt inherit money at some stage in your life.

"In Box G you have a 1, in fact, a negative 1. This means that it is a stress point and you need to take great care in this area of your life. This box stands for generosity. In this position a 1 shows that you are generous, but in your own way. You need to ensure that you actually are. If you fail to be generous when you should be, it is likely to cause problems later on. In other words, you should think carefully before saying "no." It doesn't mean that you should never say "no," of course, but you need to look at each situation carefully.

"We have another 1 in the next box. This box indicates humanitarianism. You can be very much a humanitarian, but you do it in your own way.

"Your intuition is likely to be interconnected with your entire faith and philosophy of life. Seven is a spiritual number and you have it right here in the box of intuition (Box I). You will find that your intuition will develop much more quickly if you set aside time for peace and quiet. At these times, you will grow inwardly in every possible way, growing steadily in knowledge and wisdom.

"You are happiest when you are with the people you love and care for. You have a 6, which is also your Life Path number, in Box J, which shows where you are happiest. Don't let yourself get so busy that you don't have the time you would like to be with home and family.

"You have 7 as your karmic number. This means that last time around you paid no attention to building up a faith and philosophy of life. It is important that you do work on this in this lifetime. It is likely to be a faith or philosophy that you gradually build up as you go through life.

"Box L represents love. Having a zero there doesn't mean that you will have no major love in your life. All it means is that this particular box has no particular application to this lifetime. With a 6 Life Path you will certainly enjoy the love of a wife and family, and, as you already know, you are happiest being at home with them.

"Now we come to Box M, which represents money. You have a 9 in this box. Nine is the caring, humanitarian number. It is definitely the wrong number to have here if you want to become a millionaire, as it means that you are inclined to be generous with your money. You could also work well in a humanitarian-type career.

"You have a second stress point in your chart, John. You have a negative 2 in Box N. This means that you need to ensure that you are a caring, supportive person. If you see someone doing well and succeeding, you need to enjoy that person's success, rather than resent it. It is not always easy, particularly if that person gained a position that you wanted, for instance.

"Now we come to the box of opportunities. You have a 9 here. This means that you will be given plenty of opportunities to help others. You are basically a humanitarian anyway, John, so you will enjoy all of these opportunities to help others and to make this world a better place for everyone.

"Finally, we come to your personal philosophy of life. You have a 4 in this box, John. This is the number of hard work. It shows that you do not mind working hard and long when necessary. You certainly don't expect a free lunch, and are prepared to put in all the basic groundwork. In some ways it makes you a plodder, rather than a "whizkid," but the plodder always gets there in the end."

Can you see how a yantra reading can help people understand themselves better? I always suggest that people keep their personal yantra close to them at all times, so that it can act as a good luck talisman. After they leave, they may not remember everything you told them, but will always recall how positive your reading was, and how it reflected an accurate picture of them.

Now let's learn how to part the veil a little and get a glimpse of the person's future.

chapter ten

INTO THE FUTURE

The personal yantras that we draw up give an accurate character analysis, and make wonderful protective talismans. However, they do not allow us to look at future trends. Fortunately, we can do this very easily by redrawing the yantra in a special way.

We start by placing the person's month and day of birth in Boxes A and B, as before. In Box C, instead of the last two digits of the year of birth, we place the last two digits of the year we want to look at. We then total Boxes A, B, and C and bring the result down to a single digit (except, of course, for Master Numbers) and place the result in Box D. We then complete the yantra as usual.

Let's see how Danielle, the young lady we looked at in the last chapter, will fare in 1996 (see Figure 10A).

The first thing we must realize is that six of the numbers never change. These are G, H, K, L, M, and N.

These cover the areas of generosity, humanitarianism, karma, love, money, and nurturing. How generous someone is, is not likely to change very much from year to year. Neither is their humanitarian, caring side. The karmic factors usually need a whole lifetime to be paid off, so cannot possibly alter from year to year. The love box shows the person's potential over a lifetime, rather than year by year. It would be useful to know how the money flow varied from year to year, but in the yantra we basically get a picture of how it will be earned, rather than how easily it comes. The nurturing qualities stay constant throughout life as well.

The boxes that can change are E, F, I, J, O, and P. Someone's energy and enthusiasm can definitely vary from year to year. Family and friends can change. Babies are born, people die, and our friends can change. Our intuition can also vary. Hopefully, it develops as we pass through life, but it is never a steady progression. The progressed yantra can indicate when we will make fast progress intuitively, and when we will mark time or even move back. Our opportunities vary greatly from year to year. Sometimes we can seize an opportunity and make fast progress. At other times we are held back. Family responsibilities, lack of education, and lack of time or money all affect our ability to make the most of our opportunities.

It may be a surprise to find that Box P alters every year. Our personal philosophy can and does grow and change as we progress. Naturally, the number that is in this box in the personal yantra dictates the philosophical direction the person will move in, but each year affects it as well. I remember progressing a chart for a prison inmate and finding the number 6 in this position. The number in his personal yantra was 4. The 4 indicated that his philosophy of life would gradually grow through hard work and effort. The number 6 surprised me until he told me that for the first time in his life he was enjoying counseling and helping the other inmates. He was in prison because he had taken advantage of other people, and was now learning the pleasure that can be found in helping others. The following year the philosophy number changed to a 7 and, still in prison, he embarked on a course of study.

Now, let's see how Danielle is going to fare in 1996.

"Your energy level might not be quite as high as usual," we might begin (4 in Box E). Everything you do will be accomplished with quite a bit of hard work and effort. You might be inclined to lose enthusiasm at times. Try not to let this happen. Work hard and steadily and you'll be amazed at what you can achieve during the year.

"Your home and family life will be especially close this year (6 in Box F). You will enjoy loving times with the people you care about. This is also a good year to beautify your surroundings in some way. You may decide to move house. It is a good year for close relationships. It is also a time to be careful if you do not want a baby!

"Your intuition will be a bit erratic this year (5 in Box I). You will get flashes of inspiration about all sorts of things. It will be useful to you, but it will be harder to focus than usual. You are highly intuitive anyway (she has the number 2 in this position in her personal yantra) and may get a bit frustrated that you can't direct it the way you normally can. Next year will be much easier for you in this regard. (This is because it will change to the number 6 in 1997.)

A **3**	B **12**	C **96**	D **4**
E **94**	F **6**	G **1**	H **14**
I **5**	J **97**	K **11**	L **2**
M **13**	N **0**	O **7**	P **95**

Figure 10A

"You will be doing some serious learning this year (7 in Box J). This could be spiritual, as you will be paying quite a bit of attention to that side of life this year. However, it could just as easily be study of any kind. You'll be taking it very seriously, and will thoroughly enjoy the periods you spend in study and contemplation.

"It is interesting that your best opportunities this year are in learning or spiritual areas (7 in Box O). Seize the opportunities that present themselves, work hard, and enjoy the growth and development you'll experience this year.

"Your philosophy of life this year develops with freedom and variety (5 in Box P). You'll be wanting to look at and explore a wide variety of activities. Try not to spread yourself too thin. You'll make more progress if you choose a small number of activities, rather than a dozen.

"You have an interesting year ahead, full of new and different experiences. There will be a lot of learning as well. You'll end the year with new spiritual insights. Your family life will be very close and supportive throughout the year."

Can you see how the best opportunities for Danielle gradually showed themselves?

Of course, she may not like the idea of study or spiritual growth. She might want to go out and make lots of money. She could try, and may even succeed, but the cost would be very high. She would accomplish much more by going with the flow and making the most of what the year really had to offer.

Yantras are very useful in telling us what we should be doing. They do not necessarily tell us what we want to know. However, there is a time for everything. If Danielle works hard this year and does the things her progressed yantra tells her, she will gain enormously in every area of her life. She will grow throughout 1996 and will make excellent progress in the areas favored.

If she fights against them, her progress will be slow, difficult, and incredibly frustrating.

The trends indicate what we should be doing, rather than what we will be doing. Our free will is wonderful, and life would be very unexciting without it. It would definitely be smoother, as well! The progressed yantra is a template, telling us how to make the most progress in any given period of time.

Let's look at another example, this time one with negative numbers in it. We'll do one for a man named Mark who was born on June 7, 1934. We are curious to see what the year 2000 will be like (see Figure 10B).

As you know, we place the last two digits of the year in Box C. In the year 2000 the last two numbers are both zeros. Consequently, we place a zero in Mark's progressed yantra. We then create a sum from the month and day of his birth, plus the year we are looking at:

$$
\begin{array}{r}
6 \\
7 \\
\underline{2000} \\
\end{array}
$$

2013 and 2+0+1+3 = 6.

We place the number 6 in Mark's Box D.

Now we can interpret his chart for the year 2000.

"This year is going to be very much a home and family year for you, Mark," we might begin. (This is because of the 6 in Box D.) "You may find that someone close to you needs a bit of extra help and attention. You may give advice or counsel to someone you care about. Certainly, you'll be taking part in many family activities this year.

"You have a negative two in your box of enthusiasm and energy. You are usually highly enthusiastic, but you will have to make sure that you don't get too carried away with your flashes of intuition this year. Also, you may need to put more work than you might expect into your close relationships.

"Box F represents your family and friends. Here you have an 8, which is the money number. You could benefit financially from your family or friends this year. It is much more likely, though, that you will be asked to spend money on people you care about. (As Mark is also in a 6 year, which relates to home and family, the money he spends will definitely concern his loved ones in some way. This could be a wedding, or other family celebration. It may be

A 6	B 7	C 0	D 6
E -2	F 8	G 5	H 9
I 7	J 1	K 6	L 5
M 8	N 4	O 9	P -1

Figure 10B

helping a young relative get through college, or to get established in some way. It could be anything, but as it is emphasized twice in this year, it will be something major and important.)

"Box I relates to your intuition. We have already noticed how your natural enthusiasm may get in the way of your intuitive flashes this year. In this box a 7 shows that your basic spiritual or philosophical beliefs are interwoven with your intuition this year.

"The next box relates to the joys of life. This year you will get great enjoyment out of doing your own thing. It is an excellent year for hobbies and interests. It is also a good time for taking up new interests.

"Box O relates to opportunities. With a 9 in this position you will be given opportunities to help others. This is not related to your loved ones. You will be helping humanity in general in some sort of way. This is most likely to be in the immediate community, but it could be something you do on a larger scale. Be prepared to help people who need it as the year progresses.

"The final box covers your philosophy of life during the year. It is a negative number 1. During the year you will be wanting to do a number of things that interest you personally. However, you may not be able to do them because you will be very busy helping others in various ways. It is very much a home and family year, so you will be helping the people you care about. You will also be helping people in the wider community in some way too. As a result, you may have less time than you would like to do the things that you want to do. Remain calm and relaxed. Do the things you have to do, and grab odd spare moments for yourself. This negative one applies only for this year. Next year it will be behind you.

"To sum up, I feel that you are going to have a very rewarding year, even though you may not be able to do everything that you want to do. It will be a memorable year for the family as a whole, and you will be playing a major role in that."

Can you see how helpful a reading like this can be? If Mark had been planning to spend the year fishing all by himself, he can see that it will not be possible in the year 2000. Of course, he could fight all the indications and go fishing anyway, but he would feel guilty and get little pleasure out of it. He will have a much happier, more rewarding year if he follows the guidelines set out for him in his progressed yantra.

chapter eleven

LOVE AND COMPATIBILITY

As well as creating our own personal yantra and specific ones for each year, we can also create yantras to attract the things we desire. We do this by making the top row add up to whatever number we desire. If we want love, we would draw up a yantra that totalled a number that would reduce to a 2. If we wanted a family we would design a yantra that reduced down to 6. For money, the total would have to be 8. (If our personal yantra already reduces to the number we want to enhance, we use it for both purposes. For example, if we want to attract love and our personal yantra reduces to a 2, we use our personal yantra for attracting love as well as using it as a personal talisman.)

A 8	B 14	C 65	D 7
E 63	F 9	G 6	H 16
I 8	J 66	K 13	L 7
M 15	N 5	O 10	P 64

Figure 11A: Crystal's Yantra

Let's create some special yantras for Crystal, who we met in Chapter Four. Her date of birth was August 14, 1965 (see Figure 11A). Each row of her personal yantra totals 94, which reduces to a 4.

LOVE

To create a yantra that attracts love we need each row to reduce to a two. In Crystal's case we could do this by replacing the number 7 in Box D with a 5. Now (using the same formula we used to make a personal yantra), each row of her yantra adds up to 92, which reduces to the number we want (see Figure 11B). Crystal should wear this yantra until she finds the right person and falls in love.

Crystal will also have to be aware that although the new yantra totals the number she desires, four of the numbers in her personal yantra will have changed. Box F

A 8	B 14	C 65	D 5
E 63	F 10	G 6	H 16
I 9	J 66	K 13	L 7
M 15	N 5	O 11	P 64

*Figure 11B: Crystal's Yantra
to Attract Love*

changes from a 9 to a 7. When she wears this yantra she is likely to be a little bit more wary with family and friends. Box I changes from an 8 to a 6. She is likely to be more intuitive with loved ones than with money. Finally, Box O changes from a 10 to an 8. She could have more opportunities to make (and spend) money with the new yantra. Naturally, her personal yantra will always be more powerful than a yantra constructed for a specific purpose, but the potential side effects need to be evaluated carefully as well. When the changes appear to be too negative, it is a good idea to wear the personal yantra as well as the specially constructed one.

If Crystal wanted a husband and a family, she could create the right yantra by placing a 9 in Box D. This creates a total of 96, which reduces to a 6 (see Figure 11C).

A 8	B 14	C 65	D 9
E 63	F 11	G 6	H 16
I 10	J 66	K 13	L 7
M 15	N 5	O 12	P 64

Figure 11C: Crystal's Yantra for
Husband and Family

COMPATIBILITY

We can also determine the degree of compatibility between two people by examining their yantras.

First we look at the Life Path numbers, which are in Box D. Figure 11D shows the compatibility ratings for each combination. This gives us our first clue. An "A" shows that the couple are highly compatible. "B" is also compatible. With a "C" or a "D" the couple should think carefully, and explore their yantras, before entering into a long-term relationship.

After this we look at each box in turn and see if the numbers reduce down to the same digit, or are compatible.

Let's assume that Crystal has a boyfriend called Tom who was born on April 17, 1963 (see Figure 11E). He has a 22 in Box D. Crystal has a 7. Looking in Figure 11D we

Life Path Compatibilities

LIFE PATH	1	2	3	4	5	6	7	8	9	11	22
1	B	C	D	A	A	C	A	B	D	D	C
2	C	B	B	A	C	A	B	D	B	B	A
3	D	B	A	C	C	A	C	A	A	C	B
4	A	A	C	B	D	B	A	A	D	C	B
5	A	C	C	D	B	C	C	D	B	B	C
6	C	A	A	B	C	A	C	C	A	B	D
7	A	B	C	A	C	C	B	D	C	B	A
8	B	D	A	A	D	C	D	C	C	B	A
9	D	B	A	D	B	A	C	C	A	B	B
11	D	B	C	C	B	B	B	B	B	B	A
22	C	A	B	B	C	D	A	A	B	A	B

Figure 11D

see that 7 and 22 are highly compatible. This gives us a good start.

Now we look at the other boxes in turn. In Box E Crystal has a 9 and Tom a 7. Tom is likely to put a great deal of enthusiasm and energy into solitary pursuits, such as learning and growing in knowledge and wisdom. Crystal is likely to pour her energy into helping others.

In Box F Crystal has a 9 and Tom a 6. Both of these are humanitarian numbers, so both will be interested in family life and in helping others.

Box G shows a 6 for Crystal and a 2 for Tom. Both are likely to be generous in similar ways: Crystal with family and Tom with the people he cares about.

Box H contains a 7 for Crystal and a 1 for Tom. When Crystal is helping others, she is likely to do it with spiritual

A 4	B 17	C 63	D 22
E 61	F 24	G 2	H 19
I 23	J 64	K 16	L 3
M 18	N 1	O 25	P 62

Figure 11E

motives. Tom is likely to do it with his own needs in mind, or perhaps because he simply wants to.

Box I shows that Crystal gets flashes of intuition when it comes to making or spending money. Tom's intuition is likely to be freewheeling, and he could get feelings about a wide variety of things.

Box J is an important one for compatibility, as this shows what the person most enjoys doing. Crystal enjoys having fun and expressing herself. Tom, on the other hand, is happiest when he is doing his own thing, and this may not include anyone else.

Box K shows that in a past life Crystal did not work very hard, and that Tom did not develop spiritually. (Many authorities claim that a karmic 7 is an indication of illicit love affairs in a past life that caused pain or suffering to others.[1])

Box L is also important for compatibility. When Crystal is in love it is almost spiritual. It is a quiet, gentle feeling. Tom enjoys being in love and is much more exuberant.

In Box M Crystal has a 6 and Tom a 9. Both have the ability to make money out of things they find attractive. Crystal would be happy working in a family business. Both need to ensure that they are not overly generous with their money.

Box N contains a 5 in Crystal's yantra and a 1 in Tom's. Crystal is capable of looking after a wide range of different things and nursing them all along. Tom prefers to nurture one thing at a time, and it will be something he starts himself.

Box O represents opportunities. Crystal will be given opportunities to stand on her own two feet and achieve a degree of independence. Tom will be given the opportunity to develop spiritually.

Crystal and Tom have different philosophies of life. Crystal wants to be independent and do her own thing. Tom wants to make some money and become financially secure.

Do you feel that Crystal and Tom are compatible? Their Life Path shows a high rating, but there are no boxes with numbers in common. Boxes F, G, and M contain compatible numbers, but frequently the other numbers reveal that they are poles apart. Crystal and Tom should think very carefully before entering a permanent relationship.

Incidentally, I feel that even the most unlikely of combinations can work if there is love and goodwill on both sides. However, the more there is in common, the easier it is to sustain a relationship, particularly through difficult times.

A 6	B 27	C 74	D 9
E 72	F 11	G 4	H 29
I 10	J 75	K 26	L 5
M 28	N 3	O 12	P 73

Figure 11F: Sarah's Chart

Here is another example. Sarah was born on June 27, 1974 (see Figure 11F). She has two boyfriends. One is more demanding and more ambitious than the other. She thinks he will end up being the wealthier of the two. But the other one is more fun to be with, and they certainly have much more in common. Bill was born on March 14, 1973 (see Figure 11G), and Joe was born on September 18, 1974 (see Figure 11H).

Before reading further, see if you can determine which of these two young men would make the better partner for Sarah. Look first at the Life Paths (Box D), and then go through each of the boxes in turn. You will find a clear picture gradually unfolds.

Compatibility Between Sarah and Bill

Sarah has a 9 Life Path. Her lesson in life is to become a humanitarian. Bill has a 1 Life Path. He needs to stand on

A 3	B 14	C 73	D 1
E 71	F 3	G 1	H 16
I 2	J 74	K 13	L 2
M 15	N 0	O 4	P 72

Figure 11G: Bill's Chart

his own two feet and achieve something. Looking at Figure 11D, we see that this is the most unlikely combination for success. All the same, we know that difficult combinations can succeed if both people are prepared to work at it.

In Box E Sarah has a 9. She puts enthusiasm and energy into helping others. Bill puts his enthusiasm and energy into making (or spending) money.

Sarah has a Master Number in Box F. Her family and friends are very special to her, but they sometimes fail to live up to her high expectations. She is sometimes upset with her own lack of perfection. Bill has a 3 in this box. He loves being with family and friends and can express himself very easily in this environment.

With a 4 in Box G, Sarah can put a great deal of hard work into helping others. Bill is generous in his own way.

Sarah has another Master Number in Box H (29 reduces to 11). She is inclined to be idealistic and pictures

A 9	B 18	C 74	D 3
E 72	F 5	G 7	H 20
I 4	J 75	K 17	L 8
M 19	N 6	O 6	P 73

Figure 11H: Joe's Chart

a perfect world. She is a humanitarian, but may find it difficult to be in places where there is pain and suffering. Bill's humanitarianism is connected with his faith. He will be more detached than Sarah in this area.

Sarah will have to develop her intuition primarily on her own. Bill's intuition is more natural. He may regard it as a hunch, rather than ESP, but it will come easily to him.

Sarah is happiest when simply having fun. This could be hobbies, interests, and spending time talking with friends. Bill has a Master Number in Box J, so will be happiest when doing things that he feels are important. He will have many dreams and must evaluate them carefully before acting on them as they will not all be practical.

In Box K Sarah has an 8. She misused money in a past lifetime, so must ensure that she handles it wisely this time. Bill has a 4. He was lazy in a past life, and must make sure that he works harder this time.

Sarah has a 5 in Box L. The right love relationship for her is not one that completely overpowers and stifles her. She will always need a little bit of room for herself. Bill has a 2. This means the right relationship will be an important, long-lasting one that is mutually sharing and supportive.

With a 1 in Box M, Sarah is prepared to work hard to make money. Bill has a 6, so is likely to benefit financially from his family.

Sarah will nurture her hobbies and interests with a 3 in Box N. She will foster her friendships, and seek opportunities to be with people she likes. Bill has a zero in this box. This does not mean that he nurtures nothing. Rather, it shows that this is not of great importance to him. When necessary, he will nurture things that are likely to benefit him, but otherwise his efforts are used elsewhere.

Finally, in Box P Sarah has a 1. Her philosophy of life is based on achieving independence and standing on her own two feet. Bill's philosophy of life (which is most unlikely to be obvious early on in life) is one of helping others.

Compatibility Between Sarah and Joe

Again we start by looking at the Life Path numbers. Sarah has a 9 and Joe a 3. This is an excellent combination.

In Box E, both Sarah and Joe have a 9. This means their enthusiasms and energy will be directed in the same areas.

When it comes to family and friends, Sarah has a Master Number making her rather idealistic. The people she cares about are very special. Joe has a 5 in Box F. He loves his family and friends, but also needs some freedom. He does not want to be tied down by family expectations.

Even in marriage, Joe will need a certain amount of freedom.

When Sarah is feeling generous, she is prepared to put a great deal of hard work and effort into it. Joe is likely to be generous with things that are related to his spiritual values.

With humanitarianism, Sarah has an 11, a Master Number. Joe has a 2. Both Sarah and Joe are caring people and think along the same lines. Sarah is likely to be more idealistic than Joe, but they work well together.

Both Sarah and Joe will have to work at developing and trusting their intuition. In Sarah's case it will come about through her own efforts. Joe will have to put a great deal of hard work into developing his. With a 3 Life Path, he is likely to be highly logical, and may find it hard to trust his quiet, inner voice.

Sarah and Joe both have a 3 for expressing the joys of life. They both enjoy light-hearted, carefree times with people they like. They will have a great deal of fun together.

In a past life both of them misused money. This time around they will have to ensure that they handle their money wisely. This is a lesson they can learn together. They may want to have a past life regression to see if they were together in a previous incarnation.

Sarah always needs a bit of space around her, even with the right partner. Joe has an 8 in Box L. He can make money with his partner, and/or spend money on his partner. Sarah has a 5 in Box L. This is the number of self-employment. Five and 8 harmonize very well, so Sarah and Joe would do well in business. Many couples find it hard to both live and work together.

In Box M, Sarah and Joe again have the same number—a 1. This means that they both have a desire to make money and become independent. They are on the same wavelength here.

Sarah has a 3 in Box N. She enjoys bolstering and supporting her friends, and her hobbies and interests. Joe has a 6 here. He will make an excellent father, supporting and encouraging his children, as well as the other people he cares for. As both 3 and 6 are creative numbers, Sarah and Joe would be very supportive of each other's artistic interests.

The same thing applies with Box O, as again Sarah has a 3 and Joe a 6. They both have opportunities to express themselves, help others, and develop creatively.

Finally, we look at Box P. Both Sarah and Joe have a 1 here. They both have a philosophy of life that involves standing on their own two feet and looking after themselves, ultimately achieving independence.

Would Sarah be happier with Bill or Joe? In this example I have deliberately made it rather obvious, and I hope you decided on Joe.

Sarah's relationship with Bill had very little going for it. Even the Life Paths were a difficult combination. Not one of the other boxes were the same, or even highly compatible.

Compare this with the relationship between Sarah and Joe. The Life Paths are compatible, giving a good start. Boxes E, J, K, M, and P are the same, giving a mutual outlook in these areas of life. Box H is compatible, too (11 and 2; 11 can be seen as a "super" 2). Also the numbers in Boxes L, N, and O are compatible.

A 15	B 45	C 148	D 12
E 143	F 16	G 11	H 49
I 14	J 150	K 43	L 13
M 47	N 9	O 18	P 146

Figure 111: Composite Yantra

This does not mean that Sarah will necessarily have a wonderful life with Joe. However, the chances are that she will. If she settled down with Bill, both of them would have to work extremely hard at making the relationship work. If she put anywhere near the same amount of work into her relationship with Joe, and he did the same, they would have a stable, long-lasting, happy life together.

Composite Yantra

Two people planning a permanent relationship together can create a special composite yantra to strengthen their union. Both of them should either wear it, or carry it with them at all times.

We'll use Sarah and Joe as our example. Sarah has the number 6 in Box A of her natal yantra. Joe has 9. We add the 6 and the 9 together, and place this number in Box A of a new yantra (see Figure 11I). We then place number 45 in square B, as Sarah has 27 in her Box B and Joe has 18 (27+18 = 45).

We continue on this way with each box until the yantra is complete. The numbers are not reduced in any way. The two numbers are added together and the total is inserted into the new yantra.

This yantra is never interpreted. It is simply worn as a talisman, a good luck charm, and as a permanent token of the couple's love for each other. As a result, it is normally engraved on silver or gold, rather than simply drawn on paper. If it is drawn on paper, it is then usually kept inside a gold or silver locket.

chapter twelve

MONEY

Eight is the money number, as you know by now. People who wish to attract more money to them can benefit by wearing a yantra that adds up to this number. Let's suppose Crystal decides that she wants more money. She could construct a suitable yantra by placing either the number 2 (see Figure 12A) or 11 in Box D. If she chose 11 she would need to be aware that although it makes superior attainment possible, it can also create daydreaming about money. In other words, she could make a great deal of money, or none at all.

In fact, we could place any number in Box D that reduces down to the number we desire. For instance, in Crystal's yantra to attract money, we could place the following numbers in Box D: 2, 11, 29, 38, 47, 56, 65, 74, 83, or 92. Interestingly, all of these numbers reduce down to an 11.

A 8	B 14	C 65	D 2
E 63	F 4	G 6	H 16
I 3	J 66	K 13	L 7
M 15	N 5	O 5	P 64

Figure 12A

We do not have to limit ourselves to one- or two-digit numbers. We could just as easily use a three- or four-digit number, if desired. There is usually no advantage in doing this though, as the numbers that change (Boxes F, I, and O) always reduce down to create the same single digit.

The exception is where a Master Number (an 11 or 22) is created. When this happens it is important to decide carefully whether or not to use it. A Master Number creates greater potential, but also greater responsibilities. The vibrations are stronger and more powerful. Not everyone can harness them effectively.

Sometimes people use higher numbers in Box D for aesthetic purposes. When the number in Box C is a large one, many people prefer to have another large number in Box D. Everyone born since 1950 has a large number in Box C. It is simply a matter of personal preference.

By creating and using a yantra that totals (or reduces down to) a certain number, we are attracting the essence of that number to us. The whole point of making a yantra that totals 8 is to attract money.

However, we also need to examine the numbers that have changed (Boxes F, I, and O) to see how they are affected.

In Crystal's case, Box F has changed from 9 to 4. This means that she will be very busy and will have less time to help the people she cares about. If this is going to be a problem, she will have to think carefully before using her money yantra.

Box I changes from 8 to 3. Her natal yantra showed that she got flashes of intuition concerning money. That will be blocked, as it is replaced with a 3, which is the number of logic. She is likely to lose access to part of her intuitive side. If her intuitive feelings related to spending money, rather than making it, it might even be a good thing for this to be partially blocked.

Finally, Box O changes from 1 to 5. She will lose a degree of independence, but will gain the freedom and versatility that 5 offers. She might be able to make better use of her opportunities, as 1 is more rigid in its approach than 5. The risk of 5 is that she might dabble and try and do too many different things.

All of these things need to be considered when constructing a money yantra. Money yantras are not usually interpreted. Naturally, you need to ensure that you are gaining the most suitable numbers when you first construct it. However, once it is made, it is simply worn to attract money, and the individual boxes are not read.

A 9	B 72	C 8	D 8
E 8	F 9	G 7	H 62
I 77	J 27	K 8	L 1
M 7	N 5	O 79	P 74

Figure 12B

A 1	B 14	C 11	D 8
E 12	F 7	G 2	H 13
I 6	J 9	K 19	L 3
M 15	N 4	O 5	P 10

Figure 12C

A 7	B 2	C 56	D 49
E 53	F 52	G 3	H 6
I 1	J 8	K 50	L 55
M 44	N 5	O 4	P 43

Figure 12D

What do you do if you are not happy with the changes in your numbers when you create a money yantra? There are two possibilities.

You could draw up a Square of Jupiter and wear that with your own personal yantra. Francis Barrett, in 1801, wrote that the Square of Jupiter "conduces to gain riches and favor, love, peace and concord, and to appease enemies, and to confirm honors, dignities, and counsels."[1]

Alternatively, you could wear a yantra designed for a specific financial purpose.

If you are in business and want it to improve, a special yantra (see Figure 12B) is constructed and kept on the business premises. Notice the number of 8s in this yantra.

To gain promotion at work, and thus earn more money, you should construct a special yantra (see Figure 12C) on a Tuesday.

An interesting yantra (see Figure 12D) is supposed to be written on the leaf of a cabbage. It is then believed that all of your desires, including money, will be granted.[2]

I have known people to wear several different money yantras at the same time, believing that if you wear more yantras, more money comes in. I am not convinced that this is the case. I recommend to people that they wear their own personal yantra and a single money yantra, ideally one constructed from their day and month of birth. Alternatively, I suggest that they wear the Square of Jupiter along with their personal yantra. A very attractive pendant can be made with a different yantra on each side. By wearing one of these you will be attracting good things to you from your personal yantra on one side, and also money from the money yantra on the other side.

chapter thirteen

YANTRAS IN INDIA

Yantras in India are usually drawn on paper or engraved on metal. They are then either worn or placed where it is felt they will do most good. The magic-square yantras are used either to aid meditation or as talismans to attract whatever is wanted. They are powerful energy patterns which are regarded as being the personification of God. By constructing a specific yantra, you are communicating directly with the life-force in the universe. Consequently, it is believed that if you are sincere in your request, your desires will be granted.

Yantras can be constructed for all sorts of purposes, good and bad. For instance, in India it is believed that the right yantra can cure piles, cause painless childbirth, or annoy an enemy. Not all of these are perfect magic squares.

24762	24768	24771	25320
24770	24758	24763	25341
24759	24773	24766	25325
24767	24761	24760	25344

Figure 13A

7753	177	408	7355
7754	157	1530	17750
17749	177	156	17751

Figure 13B

Usually, mantras are spoken or some sort of ritual is involved when using them.

A good example of using a yantra with a ritual is the yantra constructed to infatuate others (men, women, animals, spirits or demons). This yantra is inscribed or

50	53	56	43
55	44	49	54
45	58	51	48
52	47	46	57

Figure 13C

drawn on a gold plate. Gruel is placed on the plate each day as an offering. For forty-five days the person who constructed the yantra must gaze at it while reciting the following mantra, one thousand times each day:

Tanuc-chayabhis to taruma-tarami-Sri-dharamibhir diream Sarvan vrrvein areemima-nimagnan Smarati yah. Bhavanty arya trasyad-vama-Rarima-Salima-nayanah Sahorvasya Kati Kati na girvama-gami kah.

The ritual is simpler than this in most cases. For instance, if a woman is searching for a husband a special yantra is prepared (see Figure 13A). This yantra is drawn onto a china plate with a crayon. The yantra is then washed off the plate with water, which the woman then drinks. (Whenever possible, this yantra should be written with a special ink known as *Ashat Gandh*. This is a mixture of several items, the most important of which is water from the Ganges.)

7	2	55	48
51	52	3	6
1	8	48	54
3	50	5	4

Figure 13D

There is a special yantra for people who feel that others are talking behind their back (see Figure 13B). It can also be used if others have hurt you in some way. This yantra, known as *Swara-e-Manafakoon,* is an unusual one in a number of ways. It is 4 x 3, rather than being a perfect square. The numbers in it are three, four, and five digits long, and one of the numbers is repeated. People who use it must recite the numbers 160 times, and then keep the yantra with them to prevent a reoccurrence.

It is interesting that virtually every Indian book on the subject says that yantras should be drawn up for beneficial purposes only. However, they then go on to include yantras designed to make your enemies impotent, to break up relationships, and to make people of the opposite sex do whatever you wish.

There are a large number of all-purpose yantras, such as the one shown in Figure 13C. It must be worn around

4	9	2
3	5	7
8	1	6

Figure 13E

the neck to attract love and friendship. It is often engraved on copper or stainless steel.

The yantra in Figure 13D has to be engraved on a copper plate and worn around the neck. It is reputed to increase wealth and gain respect from others.

The 3 x 3 magic square of Wu is used in a number of variations in India. The yantra in Figure 13E is reputed to create love between two people. This yantra has to be drawn on a Friday in the hour of Venus. Both people keep a copy of the yantra with them at all times.

Another version of the 3 x 3 square is designed to create harmony between a man and a woman (see Figure 13F). This yantra should be drawn on a Wednesday or a Friday. Again, both people should keep a copy with them.

Yet another version of the 3 x 3 square is used to find missing people (see Figure 13G). It is drawn up when someone vanishes without trace. The yantra is hung from a tree and is reputed to draw the person back home.

Other 3 x 3 yantras were mentioned in Chapter One.

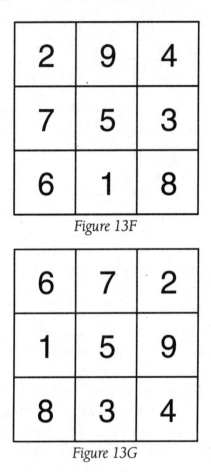

Figure 13F

Figure 13G

It is important for many of the yantras to be constructed at a special time. This is particularly so for astrological yantras which have to be made during the special hours and days set aside for the particular planet. The Table of Planetary Hours (see Figure 13H) lists the different planetary hours. The hours of the day begin at sunrise and end at sundown. Consequently, a planetary hour is not necessarily sixty minutes long. In the summer the daytime hours will be longer than sixty minutes, but in the winter they will be shorter. Naturally, the nighttime planetary hours will be shorter in summer and longer in winter.

Speaking generally:

> Yantras to attract wealth, wisdom and knowledge should be constructed and meditated upon in the hours of the sun.
>
> Yantras for divination or occult purposes should be constructed and used during the hours of the moon.
>
> Yantras relating to removing obstacles should be constructed and utilized during the hours of Mars.
>
> Yantras relating to learning and eloquence should be constructed and used during the hours of Mercury.
>
> Yantras relating to success, riches, and fame should be constructed and utilized during the hours of Jupiter.
>
> Yantras relating to love and friendship should be constructed and utilized during the hours of Venus.
>
> Yantras relating to building and practical pursuits should be constructed and utilized during the hours of Saturn.

Constructing any yantra is a profound exercise in meditation as it concentrates the mind. This is particularly the case with pictorial yantras. As the yantra is built, starting

TABLE OF PLANETARY HOURS

Hours of the Day

	Sunday	Monday	Tuesday	Wednesday	Thursday	Friday	Saturday
1	Sun	Moon	Mars	Mercury	Jupiter	Venus	Saturn
2	Venus	Saturn	Sun	Moon	Mars	Mercury	Jupiter
3	Mercury	Jupiter	Venus	Saturn	Sun	Moon	Mars
4	Moon	Mars	Mercury	Jupiter	Venus	Saturn	Sun
5	Saturn	Sun	Moon	Mars	Mercury	Jupiter	Venus
6	Jupiter	Venus	Saturn	Sun	Moon	Mars	Mercury
7	Mars	Mercury	Jupiter	Venus	Saturn	Sun	Moon
8	Sun	Moon	Mars	Mercury	Jupiter	Venus	Saturn
9	Venus	Saturn	Sun	Moon	Mars	Mercury	Jupiter
10	Mercury	Jupiter	Venus	Saturn	Sun	Moon	Mars
11	Moon	Mars	Mercury	Jupiter	Venus	Saturn	Sun
12	Saturn	Sun	Moon	Mars	Mercury	Jupiter	Venus

Hours of the Night

	Sunday	Monday	Tuesday	Wednesday	Thursday	Friday	Saturday
1	Jupiter	Venus	Saturn	Sun	Moon	Mars	Mercury
2	Mars	Mercury	Jupiter	Venus	Saturn	Sun	Moon
3	Sun	Moon	Mars	Mercury	Jupiter	Venus	Saturn
4	Venus	Saturn	Sun	Moon	Mars	Mercury	Jupiter
5	Mercury	Jupiter	Venus	Saturn	Sun	Moon	Mars
6	Moon	Mars	Mercury	Jupiter	Venus	Saturn	Sun
7	Saturn	Sun	Moon	Mars	Mercury	Jupiter	Venus
8	Jupiter	Venus	Saturn	Sun	Moon	Mars	Mercury
9	Mars	Mercury	Jupiter	Venus	Saturn	Sun	Moon
10	Sun	Moon	Mars	Mercury	Jupiter	Venus	Saturn
11	Venus	Saturn	Sun	Moon	Mars	Mercury	Jupiter
12	Mercury	Jupiter	Venus	Saturn	Sun	Moon	Mars

Figure 13H

from the *bindu*, the adept meditates briefly on every line he or she adds. It is not unusual for people to enter a trance-like state as they construct a yantra. In this way they enter the very center of the yantra and become one with it. I vividly remember watching a man draw a yantra in the earth outside the famous Red Fort in New Delhi. He was totally absorbed in what he was doing, and was unaware of the thousands of people and the incredible noise going on around him.

chapter fourteen

TALISMANS

As we have seen, yantras are often worn as talismans to attract to the wearer whatever he or she desires. Talismans have been made and worn since time immemorial to protect and strengthen the wearer. Their power is increased if made at the right time or from the right materials.

They are still as popular today as they have been at any other time in our history. People carry a wide variety of amulets and talismans. It might be a "lucky" rabbit's foot. It could be a four-leaf clover. Maybe a lock of hair belonging to someone special. It could even be mustard seeds, encased in plastic, to remind the wearer of Jesus' words about the growth of the Kingdom of Heaven. These things are all regarded as lucky talismans. Many people have a St. Christopher medal in their cars, as he is regarded as the patron saint of travellers. It is a talisman. Even cigarette cases or money clips can be regarded as talismans after they have been carried for a while. People can derive confidence and other positive energies from touching or carrying talismans.

Amulets are usually worn touching the skin and are visible to others. Talismans are not usually displayed. They are kept in a pocket or purse, or worn on a cord around the neck. It does not matter if they are seen by others, but that is not their purpose. Ideally, both amulets and talismans should be kept as close to the body as possible. The words "talisman" and "amulet" have come to mean the same thing. Originally, talismans were worn to attract to the person what he or she wanted. Amulets were worn to ward off negative influences.

Some of the oldest amulets are rings and they were believed to provide strength, power, and happiness. The wedding ring on the third finger is part of a very ancient tradition. Originally, a ring was worn on the index finger to tell others that the person wanted to get married. A ring on the middle finger told everyone that the person was in love. And a ring on the third (ring) finger told everyone that the person was engaged or married.[1]

Back in the 1960s, when the United States Navy was attempting to send Vanguard rockets into orbit, and failing, the contractors claimed the failure was due to the absence of St. Christopher medals. Sure enough, the very first rocket that was sent out with a St. Christopher medal worked perfectly.[2]

Virtually nothing is known about St. Christopher, other than that he lived in Asia Minor in the third century and was martyred by the Romans. However, there are many stories about him. One of these relates that he was a

1	2	3	4	5	6	7	8	9
A	B	C	D	E	F	G	H	I
J	K	L	M	N	O	P	Q	R
S	T	U	V	W	X	Y	Z	

Figure 14A

soldier who wanted to serve the most powerful ruler in the world. He found one, but soon discovered that he was scared of Satan. Christopher then switched his allegiance to Satan, only to find that he, too, had a weakness; Satan was scared of the sign of the cross. Christopher finally transferred his allegiance to Christ and decided to spend the rest of his life helping others. He did this by settling on the side of a dangerous river and ferrying people across to the other side. No one drowned the whole time Christopher lived there.[3]

As talismans of all sorts are still being used frequently in the West, it should be no surprise to learn of their popularity in the East.

Yantras are worn or carried as talismans for a wide variety of purposes. They are also used to make sigils, which are numerological signatures, drawn or engraved upon the yantra. A sigil is believed to contain the essential essence of the person and the square it is constructed on. Sigils are usually made from the name the person is generally known by. If Charles is normally known as Chuck, we would create his sigil using "Chuck."

We can consult Figure 14A to turn our name into numbers: for example, by turning my first name, Richard, into numbers I get: 9, 9, 3, 8, 1, 9, and 4. I can now enter these into any magic square I wish. For instance, as I am a

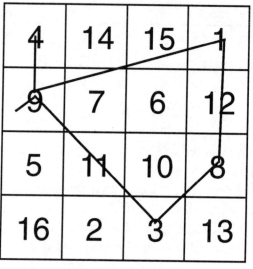

Figure 14B

Sagittarian, I might choose to place it on the Square of Jupiter (see Figure 14B). (This is because Jupiter is the ruling planet of Sagittarius.)

I start by placing my pen on the number 9. As my name contains this number twice in a row, I make a small sideways movement to indicate the two 9s. I then draw a line down to the number 3, up to the 8, the 1, and back to 9, before finishing on the 4. This creates my personal sigil for the Square of Jupiter.

I can carry this around with me, as the magic square has even more power attached to it, now that I have personalized it. Alternatively, I may choose to have some jewelry made in the shape of the sigil. If you are good with your hands, you may be able to do this yourself, using fine gold or silver wire.

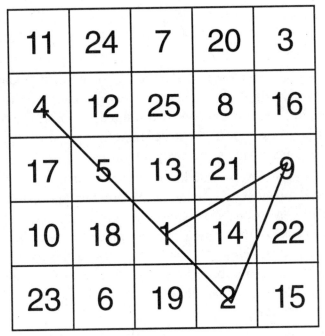

Figure 14C

Here is another example (see Figure 14C). Debra wants a sigil on the Square of Mars to help cure a lingering illness.

She begins by turning her name into numbers: 4, 5, 2, 9, and 1. Now she starts drawing from the square containing number 4. Number 5 is right next to it, so she draws a line connecting them. Her next number is 2, and the line continues diagonally down to this square. This means that number 5 is not specifically indicated, as the line appears to go directly from number 4 to number 2. However, as the line goes right through number 5, it is regarded as being indicated in her personal sigil. She now draws a line from number 2 up to 9, and then back to 1 to complete her sigil.

As she has constructed it for health reasons she should place the sigil as close as possible to the affected part of her body.

It is also possible to create sigils of other people's names and apply them to a magic square. For instance, if you were in love with someone and wanted the love to be reciprocated, you could construct the other person's sigil on the Square of Venus and carry it with you.

In the West, medieval writers such as Abbot Trithemius, Peter de Abano, and Cornelius Agrippa wrote extensively on magic squares and sigils as they applied in the Europe of their day. Their interpretations came from a study of the Kabbalah, and demonstrated the incredible importance of numbers in this system. The Indian tradition grew along similar lines and is still used frequently today.

Another popular talisman is the one created from the word "Abracadabra." Legend has it that this word was invented by Serenus Samonicus, physician to Emperor Caracalla, but it is believed to have been known long before his time.[4] An ancient Chaldean saying, "Abbada Ke Dabra," meaning "perish like the word," is a more likely origin of the apparently nonsense word. Each line of the talisman was originally said out loud, and, as the word diminished, so did the illness. In India today, it is worn to bring good luck and to protect whoever wears it from evil spirits.

It is interesting to compare the Western and Eastern versions of this talisman. In the West, the last letter is removed each time. In the East, both the first and last letters are removed (see Figure 14C). This means that the

ABRACADABRA
ABRACADABR
ABRACADAB
ABRACADA
ABRACAD
ABRACA
ABRAC
ABRA
ABR
AB
A

Western version of ABRACADABRA

ABRACADABRA
BRACADABR
RACADAB
ACADA
CAD
A

Eastern version of ABRACADABRA

Figure 14C

word "Abracadabra" can be read by reading down the left side and up the right.

Why do talismans work? The most obvious explanation is that if people believe they will work, they subconsciously attract to them what they desire. The talisman gives them confidence and enables them to achieve things that couldn't have occurred otherwise. However, this doesn't explain how talismans still work for people who have no faith in them. It would seem that talismans have a life of their own, and put out energies that create the desired results. This accords perfectly with the Indian belief that yantras not only represent God, but are also a home for God.

chapter fifteen

CONCLUSION

I hope you found this introduction to yantras interesting and useful. I have found them of enormous help in my own life. I have constructed thousands of them for my clients over the years and have had wonderful feedback about their effectiveness. The people I have taught this system to all report similar results.

You may wish to draw them up for divination purposes or to attract love, money, and happiness. You may wish to create talismans from them to create a magnet that draws good things to you. Use them with respect. I have deliberately left the negative yantras out of this book. I believe they should be used only to help people, and never to hurt.

ENDNOTES

Introduction

1. Mathers, S. L. MacGregor, translator. *The Book of the Sacred Magic of Abramelin the Mage by Abraham the Jew.* John M. Watkins, London, second edition, 1900. This book is currently available from Dover Publications, Inc., 180 Varick Street, New York, NY, 10014.

Chapter 1

1. Mookerjee, Ajit, and Madhu Khanna. *The Tantric Way.* Thames and Hudson Ltd., London, 1977, p. 56. This book also contains a clear explanation of the symbology of the Shri Yantra, pp. 57–62.

2. Chawdhri, Dr. L. R. *Practicals of Mantras and Tantras.* Sagar Publications, New Delhi, 1985, pp. 6–9.

3. Breaux, Charles. *Journey into Consciousness.* Nicholas-Hays, Inc., York Beach, Maine, 1989, p. 195.

4. Braha, James T. *Ancient Hindu Astrology for the Modern Western Astrologer.* Hermetician Press, Miami, Florida, 1986, p.73. This book also includes the correct mantras for each planet.

Chapter Two

1. Andrews, W. S. *Magic Squares and Cubes.* Open Court Publishing, New York, NY, 1917, pp. 18–44. Republished by Dover Publications, New York, NY, 1960.

Chapter 3

1. Emperor Wu of Hsia is known by a number of names. Apart from Wu, the most popular version of his name is Fu Hsi.

2. Groves, Derham. *Feng-Shui and Western Building Ceremonies.* Graham Brash, Singapore, and Tynron Press, Scotland, 1991, p. 6.

3. Further information on oracle bones can be found in: *The Birth of China*, Herrlee Glessner, Frederick Ungar Publishing, New York, NY, 1937; *Bone Culture of Ancient China*, William Charles White, University of Toronto Press, Toronto, 1945; *Fifty Years of Study in Oracle Bone Inscriptions,* Tso-pin Tung, Center for East Asian Cultural Studies, 1964; and *Sources of Shang History,* David N. Keightley, University of California Press, 1978.

4. Hulse, David Allen. *The Key of it All.* Llewellyn Publications, St Paul, Minnesota, 1994, "Sixth Key."

5. Culling, Louis. *The Pristine Yi King.* Llewellyn Publications, St Paul, Minnesota, 1989, pp. 2–6.

6. Walters, Derek. *The Alternative I Ching*. The Aquarian Press, Northamptonshire, 1987, p. 45. This book was originally published in 1983 as *The T'ai Hsüan Ching*.

7. Culling, Louis. *The Pristine Yi King*. Ibid., p. 3.

8. Walters, Derek. *The Alternative I Ching*. Ibid., pp. 44–50. The nine magic squares are also shown in pages 201–205.

9. de Kermadec, Jean-Michel Huon. *The Way to Chinese Astrology*. Unwin Paperbacks, London, 1983, pp. 17–18.

10. Skinner, Stephen. *The Living Earth Manual of Feng-Shui*. Routledge and Kegan Paul Ltd., London, 1982. Republished by Graham Brash, Singapore, 1983, pp. 65–67.

11. Coates, Austin. *Numerology*. Citadel Press, Secaucus, New Jersey, 1974.

12. Templeton, Hettie. *Numbers and Their Influence*. DeVorss and Company, Marina del Rey, California, 1940.

13. Line, Julia. *The Numerology Workbook*. The Aquarian Press, Wellingborough, 1985, p. 74.

14. de Kermadec, Jean-Michel Huon. *The Way to Chinese Astrology*. Ibid., p. 13.

Chapter Eleven

1. Goodwin, Matthew Oliver. *Numerology: The Complete Guide (Volume 1)*. Newcastle Publishing Company, Inc., North Hollywood, California, 1981, p. 311.

Chapter Twelve

1. Barrett, Francis. *The Magus*. Lackington, Allen and Company, London, 1801, p. 143. There are many

editions of this classic work available. Mine is a facsimile edition published by The Aquarian Press, Wellingborough, 1989.

2. Chawdhri, Dr. L. R. *Practicals of Yantras*. Sagar Publications, New Delhi, 1984, p. 128.

Chapter Fourteen

1. Larner, Saul P. *Astrological Assistance*. Prentice-Hall, Inc., Englewood Cliffs, New Jersey, 1974, p. 143.

2. Day, Harvey. *Occult Illustrated Dictionary*. Oxford University Press, New York, NY, 1976, p. 129.

3. Brasch, R. *Strange Customs*. David McKay Co Inc., New York, 1976. Reprinted by Tynron Press, Scotland, 1990, pp. 181–183.

4. Lippman, Deborah, and Paul Colin. *How to Make Amulets, Charms and Talismans*. M. Evans and Company, Inc, New York, NY, 1974, p. 120.

BIBLIOGRAPHY AND SUGGESTED READING

Magic Squares

Andrews, W. S. *Magic Squares and Cubes*. Dover Publications, New York, 1960. Originally published by Open Court Publishing Company, 1917.

Hulse, David Allen. *The Key of it All*. Llewellyn Publications, St Paul, Minnesota, 1994.

Barrett, Francis. *The Magus*. First published 1801. Numerous versions still available, including a facsimile edition published by The Aquarian Press, Wellingborough, 1989.

Mandalas

Dahlke, Rudiger. *Mandalas of the World*. Sterling Publishing Company, New York, NY, 1992.

Argüelles, José, and Miriam Argüelles. *Mandala*. Shambhala Publications, Inc., Boston and London, 1972.

Yantras

Johari, Harish. *Tools for Tantra*. Destiny Books, Vermont, 1986.

The I Ching

Riseman, Tom. *Introduction to the I Ching*. The Aquarian Press, Wellingborough, 1980.

Culling, Louis. *The Pristine Yi King*. Llewellyn Publications, St. Paul, Minnesota, 1989.

Hwa, Jou, Tsung. *The Tao of I Ching*. Tai Chi Foundation, Piscataway, New Jersey, 1984.

The T'ai Hsüan Ching

Walters, Derek. *The Alternative I Ching*. The Aquarian Press, Wellingborough, 1987.

Feng-Shui

Groves, Derham. *Feng-Shui and Western Building Ceremonies*. Graham Brash (Pte) Limited, Singapore, and Tynron Press, Scotland, 1991.

Eitel, Ernest J. *Feng-Shui*. Originally published by Trubner and Company, 1873. Reprinted by Graham Brash (Pte) Limited, Singapore, 1985.

Skinner, Stephen. *The Living Earth Manual of Feng-Shui*. Routledge and Kegan Paul Limited, London, 1982. Reprinted by Graham Brash (Pte) Limited, Singapore, 1983.

The Ki

Yoshikawa, Takashi. *The Ki*. St. Martin's Press, New York, NY, 1986.

Kushi, Michio. *Nine Star Ki.* One Peaceful World Press, Becket, Massachusetts, 1991.

Sachs, Bob. *The Complete Guide to Nine Star Ki.* Element Books Ltd., Longmead, and Element, Inc. Dorset and Rockport, Massachusetts, 1992.

Kigaku

Mori, Takeo, and Dragan Milenkovic. *Secrets of Japanese Astrology.* Weatherhill, Inc., New York, NY, 1993.

Tic-Tac-Toe Numerology

Gruner, Mark, and Christopher K. Brown. *Numbers of Life.* Taplinger Publishing Company, New York, NY, 1978.

Coates, Austin. *Numerology.* Citadel Press, Secaucus, New Jersey, 1974.

Webster, Richard. *Quick Readings with Numerology.* Brookfield Press, Auckland, 1979.

Phillips, David A. *Secrets of the Inner Self.* Angus and Robertson Publishers, Sydney, 1980.

Talismans

Ophiel. *The Art and Practice of Talismanic Magic.* Samuel Weiser, Inc., York Beach, Maine, 1973.

Lippman, Deborah, and Paul Colin. *How to Make Amulets, Charms and Talismans.* M. Evans and Company, Inc, New York, NY, 1974.

Conway, David. *The Complete Magic Primer.* The Aquarian Press, Wellingborough, 1991. Originally published in 1988 as *Magic: An Occult Primer.*

INDEX

Abano, Peter de, 152

Abracadabra, 152–153

Abraham of Würzburg, xiv

Abramelin the Mage, xiv

Agrippa, Cornelius, xv, 22, 152

amulets, 147–148

Angelic Tablets, xvi

Arrow of Activity, 37

Arrow of Determination, 37–38

Arrow of Emotional Balance, 36

Arrow of Frustrations, 37

Arrow of Hypersensitivity, 37

Arrow of Poor Memory, 37

Arrow of Practicality, 36

Arrow of Skepticism, 38

Arrow of Spirituality, 37

Arrow of the Intellect, 36

Arrow of the Planner, 36

Arrow of Will Power, 37

Arrows of Pythagoras, 32

astrological yantras, 5, 142

bindu, 2, 145

Black Earth, 26

chakra, 2–3

circle, 2–3

Coates, Austin, 32

Crowley, Aleister, xv

Dee, Dr. John, xvi

destiny number, 59, 99

divination, 9, 19–21, 23, 32, 143, 155

Due of Kau, 23

Dürer, Albrecht, xv

Enochian System, xvi

feng-shui, xiii, 21, 30–31

Franklin, Benjamin, xvi

Golden Dawn (Order of), xvi

Green Tree, 27, 29

Guru bead, 5–6

Hwang Ho (River), xiii, 19

I Ching, xiii, 3, 21–22, 39

Jupiter, 5, 7–9, 135–136, 143–144, 150

Kabbalah, xiv, 152

Kelly, Sir Edward, xvi

Ketu, 5, 8

ki, xiii, 21, 23–24, 28–29, 32

Kigaku, 21

Life Path, 38, 49, 59–63, 65, 99, 102, 104, 118–119, 121–122, 125–126

Louis XIV of France, xvi

lotus, 3, 5

MacGregor Mathers, S. L., xiv

magic square, xii–xviii, 6–9, 11–16, 18–19, 21–23, 27, 30–32, 41–42, 44, 141, 149–150, 152

mandala, 1, 5

mantra, 2, 5–6, 139

master builder, 56, 64, 69

Master Number, 42–43, 56, 63, 65, 107

meditation, 1–3, 81, 137, 143

Mercury, 5, 7–8, 143–144

Moon, 5–6, 8–9, 143–144

Nav–Graha, 8-9

Negative Number, 97, 111

New Delhi, xi–xii, 145

numerological yantra, 9

old souls, 63

oracle bones, 20–21

personal yantra, 41, 43, 45, 47, 105, 108–109, 115–117, 135–136

pictorial yantra, xi, 1–2

Planes of Pythagoras, 32

plastron, 20

Purple Fire, 28–29

Pythagoras, 22, 32

Rahu, 5, 8

Red Metal, 28

Saturn, 5, 7–9, 22, 143–144

Shakti, 4

Shang calendar, 21

Shiva, 4

Shri Yantra, 4-5

sigil, 149-152

square, 3, 6–9, 11–16, 18–19, 21–24, 27, 30–32, 39, 41–42, 44–45, 129, 135–136, 140–141, 149–152

Square of Saturn, 22

stress point, 103–104

Sun, 5–6, 8, 29, 143–144

Sung dynasty, 31

Swara-e-manafakoon, 140

Tâbit ibn Quarra, xiv

T'ai Hsüan Ching, 3, 21–23, 39

talisman, xiv, 9, 45, 105, 115, 129, 147–149, 152–154

Taoist, 21

tortoise, xiii, 19–22, 30

transits, 9

triangle, 3, 5

Trithemius, Abbot, 152

Turquoise Tree, 26

Upanishads, 2

Vedic scriptures, 2

Venus, 5, 8, 141, 143–144, 152

White Earth, 28

White Metal, 27

White Water, 26, 29

Wu of Hsia, xiii, 22, 39

yang, 3, 21–23, 30–31

Yantra of the Cosmos, 4

Yellow Earth, 27

yin, 3, 21–23, 30–31

☽ REACH FOR THE MOON

AURA READING FOR BEGINNERS
Develop Your Psychic Awareness for Health & Success

Richard Webster

When you lose your temper, don't be surprised if a dirty red haze suddenly appears around you. If you do something magnanimous, your aura will expand. Now you can learn to see the energy that emanates off yourself and other people through the proven methods taught by Richard Webster in his psychic training classes.

These proven methods for seeing the aura will help you:
- Interpret the meanings of colors in the aura
- Find a career that is best suited for you
- Relate better to the people you meet and deal with
- Enjoy excellent health
- Discover areas of your life that you need to work on
- Make aura portraits with pastels or colored pencils
- Discover the signs of impending ill health, drug abuse, and pain
- Change the state of your aura and stimulate specific chakras through music, crystals, color
- See what the next few weeks or months are going to be like for you

1-56718-798-6
208 pp., 5 $^3/_{16}$ x 8, illus. $7.95

To order, call 1-800-THE MOON

Prices subject to change without notice

CHINESE NUMEROLOGY
The Way to Prosperity &
Fulfillment
Richard Webster

Chinese Numerology teaches the original system of numerology which is still practiced throughout the East, and from which Chinese astrology, feng-shui and the I Ching were all derived.

Chinese Numerology is the first book in the West to explain and teach the traditional Chinese system:

- Draw a numerology chart in a matter of seconds and be able to interpret it accurately

- Is this a money year? A good year to get married? Discover the future trends in you life by looking at your personal years, months and days

- Uncover your compatibility with another person using an easy technique that has never been published before

Includes solar-lunar conversion tables to the year 2000

1-56718-804-4
260 pp., 7 x 10

$12.95

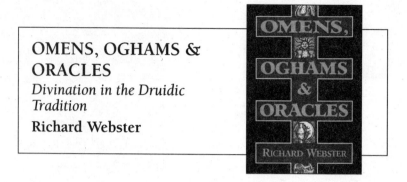